WHAT MUST I DO TO BE SAVED?

PREPARING YOUTH TO RECEIVE THE PROMISE

I D WARD

WESTBOW
PRESS
A DIVISION OF THOMAS NELSON

WestBow Press books may be ordered through booksellers or by contacting:

WestBow Press
A Division of Thomas Nelson
1663 Liberty Drive
Bloomington, IN 47403
www.westbowpress.com
1-(866) 928-1240

ISBN: 978-1-4497-5543-0 (hc)
ISBN: 978-1-4497-5541-6 (sc)
ISBN: 978-1-4497-5542-3 (e)

Library of Congress Control Number: 2012910282

Printed in the United States of America

WestBow Press rev. date: 06/20/2012

CONTENTS

PREFACE

What Must I Do To Be Saved? is the inspired word of God tailor-made for youth and spiritual babes. The text contains testimonies, exhortations, and moral lessons that portray common lifestyles of teenagers. Scriptural references provide basic fundamentals and teachings of salvation, faith, and repentance. The King James Version (KJV) of the bible is used throughout the text. Some passages may be quoted in full or in part. The scripture references may also include italics for added emphasis. Brackets may be inserted to define or clarify words and phrases that may not be easily understood by novice readers. I strongly recommend reading verses preceding and following each scripture so that the meaning can be interpreted and applied in its proper context.

The outline guides youth toward victory in Christ Jesus by heightening teens' awareness of God's presence within them. The internal battle of spirit versus flesh is identified to prepare youth to resist temptation and overcome obstacles. Each subtopic concludes with a lesson review that consists of multiple choice, true/false, and fill-in-the-blank questions. Each question has a scriptural reference to assist research and memorization of the Holy Scriptures. "Check Yourself" is provided to emphasize how the biblical teachings can be directly applied to individual circumstances, mind-set, or development.

The main idea is to teach the younger generation that God has called everyone to repent and be saved (2 Peter 3:9). The goal is to plant a seed of Christ, provide godly wisdom, train youth to see their reflection in the Bible, and recognize the voice of God within them. Then teenagers are well-equipped to make their own choice to follow Jesus Christ.

INTRODUCTION

Many critics said I was wasting my time by offering a call to salvation to high school students, juvenile delinquents, and youth such as you. Doubters suggested that spiritual development would not be received by this more violent, fast-learning Generation X of today. But I believe in you! I stand firm in serving my Lord and Savior, Jesus Christ, just as I know you can. I admit I cannot save or change anyone. However, your reading of this text confirms that all things are possible through Christ Jesus, who strengthens you and me (Philippians 4:13).

There were times I almost gave up on reaching out to youth with a higher purpose in mind. Then I read the Old Testament book of Ezekiel 2; 3:17-18. Ezekiel was a prophet and priest commissioned to be God's messenger to the children of Israel. The Israelites were God's chosen people, but they were also rebellious and hard-hearted, just like many young gang members or students with bad attitudes you may know.

> "[Ezekiel], I have made you a watchman over the house of Israel: Hear the word of my mouth, and give them warning for me. When I say to the wicked that they shall surely die; and you do not give them warning, or speak to warn the wicked from his wicked ways, to save his life; the same wicked man shall die in his iniquity [sin]; but his blood will I require at your hand," God said (Ezekiel 3:17-18, brackets added).

I accept that many young people are trapped in relationships, locked-up mind-sets, etc. This message is also for you, the model student and well-behaved teenager. By the grace of God, I have broken the chains from which Christ Jesus can also set you free. Learn from my mistakes. Today, I accept God's call to deliver a message that will save your life!

> "The wages [cost or penalty] of sin is death. But the gift of God is eternal life through Jesus Christ our Lord (Romans 6:23, brackets added)."

Please, my young sisters and brothers, I beg you to turn from your lifestyle of pride, self-will, and unwillingness to forgive. Accept God's free gift of salvation while there is still time. Today is your chance to start a new life in God's family.

> "Except a man be born again, he cannot see the kingdom of God . . . Except a man be born of water and Spirit, he cannot enter into the kingdom of God" (John 3:3, 5).

What must I do to be saved? I'm glad you asked, my dear friend! Romans 10:9-10 explains that if you " . . . confess with thy mouth the Lord Jesus, and shalt believe in thine heart that God hath raised him from the dead, thou shalt be saved"! With the heart you believe unto righteousness. With your mouth a confession is made to salvation. But there's more! Allow me to walk you through some basic steps of how to live a more peaceful, productive life for Jesus.

AUTHOR BIOGRAPHICAL NOTE

As a youth, I was raised in a two-parent home. We were lower-middle class and lived in housing projects and urban neighborhoods. However, I was taught not to be a product of my degenerate, shortsighted environment. I received spiritual guidance at church while in elementary school and was enrolled in a year-round Christian youth program called Destination Discovery. I attended magnet schools that promoted diversity, fairness in opportunity, and educational excellence.

At fifteen, I made a costly decision to indulge in the street life. I went from being an honor roll student to being a mediocre high school graduate. Then I was a half-attentive, misdirected college student not living up to my full potential. Several poor choices landed me in prison, and incarceration proved to be my Damascus experience. God brought Metamorphism Ministries to me, and I learned the effective laws of Bible study: context; normal usage of words; the Bible as a whole; and foundational truths of sound doctrine. More importantly, I learned practical application of the Bible during the most unfavorable circumstances.

My divine transformation came when I transitioned from being a loyal churchgoer to a follower of Jesus Christ. The difference was that I learned to be Christ-like in my own house too, rather than only when I was in God's house. I accepted accountability as a born-again believer and an explosion of revelation transpired as my personal relationship with Jesus became more intimate. I am on my path of restoring relationships and tearing down barriers to promote spiritual growth. My calling is to repair the breaches I created in the lives of many adolescent, as God has given me visions that will help build the younger generation into noble saints.

My goal is to share the gospel and my testimonies in a praiseworthy format applicable to the lives of youth and spiritual babes. My message from God is tailored to those who suffer the consequences of rebellion, poor decisions, relational traps, and unfavorable circumstances. By the power of the Holy Spirit, everyone can break through to success! To walk in repentance is a lifelong journey that requires discipline, patience, and faithfulness. As I am in the business of saving souls, fulfillment of my ministry manifests every time someone asks, "What must I do to be saved?"

As a published author, my objective is to be a virtuous vessel God brings forth to fulfill his promise of salvation to all people worldwide. My reward comes when true repentance is birthed in the hearts of sinners and backslidden believers. My message is more of a movement: take control by learning self-control in the pursuit of spiritual excellence! My duty is to break down barriers and build relationships to strengthen God's army with repentant souls who simply need inspiration and direction toward leadership in God's kingdom.

What Must I Do To Be Saved? The text begins with an introduction of my calling from God to deliver a message to our youth offering an opportunity to be saved from sin. My revelation and inspiration came from the scripture, Ezekiel 2; 3:17-18. I admit that I cannot change anyone, nor can I force salvation upon adolescents. However, to remain obedient to the will of God, I must pursue the mission of saving souls!

Agape,
Bro Israel

OPENING PRAYER

Dear Heavenly Father,

I come to you in the name of Jesus, asking you to pour out your mercy and grace on me as I read these lessons. Soften my heart so I can receive Jesus into my life. Increase my understanding so I can obey your word consistently. Put ministers and helpers in my life to encourage me as I do my best to overcome peer pressure and my negative thoughts. Direct me toward your purpose for my life. Dear Lord, I pray for you to teach me self-control and grant me patience, though I am young. Thank you for the victory you gave when Jesus died on the cross and conquered sin. In Jesus' name I pray. Amen (John 5:24; 1 John 5:4).

CHAPTER 1

ACCEPTING YOUR CALL TO SALVATION

When I was a youth, my pastor offered a call to salvation at the end of every church service. Most of the time, I was passing notes, eating candy, or half asleep. I had heard the story of Jesus in Sunday school. Mary was a virgin who gave birth to Jesus by the power of the Holy Spirit (Matt. 1:18-25). *The promise was that Jesus would save his people from sin,* fulfilling the Old Testament prophecy of the coming Messiah (Isaiah 7:14; Matthew 1:20-23).

Pastor Maxwell would stand in front of the congregation, inviting lost souls to give their lives to Christ. "The doors of the church are open. Come! Let Jesus be the head of your life," he said, extending his arms with a smile. I looked around, waiting for someone to take that long, intimidating walk to the front of the church. Too many of my friends were looking for me to do it. One day, I overcame my fears and submitted to that voice inside my head that urged me to go to the altar. I did not plan to accept the call to salvation, and I did not understand what gave me the strength to do so on that particular day. A minister stood with me in front of the church as she took notes about my personal information.

Sister Mikel asked me, "Are you here by confession of faith or restoration of faith?"

I shrugged my shoulders, not understanding the question. Sister Mikel explained that "confession of faith" meant that I was accepting Jesus as my Lord and Savior for the first time.

My voice cracked as I muttered, "I have been baptized at another church."

Sister Mikel smiled. "Oh, you're here by restoration of faith. You've probably backslid and need to rededicate your life to Christ."

Sister Mikel was right. Nothing about my lifestyle or attitude was Christ-like, nor had I shown any improvement. I knew I could be a better person, but I was raised in the projects. Thugs, drugs, and nonsense were all around me. The truth of the matter was that God was speaking to me at a young age concerning right from wrong. *Now* I understand that right is obedience and wrong is sin. *Then* I had to make a choice to believe the gospel or die in sin.

Sister Mikel wrapped her arms around me as she announced to the church that I was rededicating my life to Christ. The congregation rose to its feet, applauding, as my family stood by my side. Even a few elders whom I had never met came to support me. Pastor Maxwell shook my hand and saluted me as an official member of Paradise Baptist Church. Each member of my church gave me the "right hand of fellowship" by welcoming me into the body of Christ with handshakes, hugs, and pats on the back. It felt good to have so many elders, brothers, and sisters in Christ encouraging me to seek God's best, no matter how bad the projects were where I grew up.

1.1 The Fall of Adam

Why do I need to be saved? *Everyone on this earth has a need for salvation.* Romans 3:23 says "All have sinned and fall short of the glory of God." When I was a teenager, I assumed that children were so perfect and pure. Yes, a child may be innocent and not held accountable for being misled. But what about those teens that choose to disobey and rebel? Jesus said that unless you are born again—baptized of water and Spirit—you cannot enter the kingdom of heaven (John 3:3, 5).

Today you can turn to God. It's your choice to spend an eternity of glory in heaven or an eternity of torture in hell. When God first created man, he said it was very good (Genesis 1:31). The truth is, since the fall of Adam, we are all born with a sinful nature. Because of Adam and Eve's sin, humanity has adopted natural instincts to lie, deceive, and disobey. For you to better understand that we received Adam's sinful nature, let's analyze the natural birth of children.

When a baby is born, he or she inherits a mix of the parents' DNA and physical characteristics. These biological traits are passed down through every generation of the family tree. Mankind also inherited the sinful nature known as the "Adamic nature" from our first father on Earth, Adam. The Bible notes clearly that God first created man in his image and likeness (Genesis 1:27). Next, the Bible pinpoints that Adam's son, Seth, was made in his own likeness and image (Genesis 5:3). From then on until now, every child is born of a corruptible seed that can fall into temptation. Sure, some of us have a more dominant Adamic nature, which causes us to fall into sin more than others do. Even a "momma's boy," "daddy's girl," or that precious child whom everyone loves has a nature to sin and sin again. This is why we all need to be saved by the grace of God.

Moral Lesson

Let's analyze a toddler so you better understand the Adamic nature that tempts us with sin. My brother, West, was a hyperactive toddler. West would spill his milk on purpose, touch things he was not supposed to handle, and run from adults just for fun. Even when West got his hands spanked, he would stare at my parents and disobey again.

One day, West knocked a small dove off the table. I was looking directly at my little brother when he did it. When I asked, "West, did you do that?" he shook his head. At first, I assumed he was too young to fully understand yes and no. Certainly a toddler could not lie!

To test my brother's knowledge of good and evil, I offered him some candy. As I opened the wrapper, I asked, "You want some Skittles?" West's eyes widened and reached out his hand as he nodded. My little brother understood yes from no, right from wrong, even before he could speak clearly. I was confused, because no one taught him to shake his head no when he was about to get disciplined for misbehaving. At that time, I did not know that I was witnessing the Adamic nature working in my two-year-old brother. Like me, West definitely needed God to save him once he was old enough to make that decision.

Job 14:1 states, "Man that is born of a woman is a few days old and full of trouble." I'm sure that you have been around a toddler who was flat-out bad. You probably know at least one child whom everyone regrets having to babysit because he or she is too disobedient. God warned mankind that, because of our natural instincts to sin, we all fall short. Paul writes in Romans 6:23, "The wages of sin is death: but the gift of God is eternal life in Christ Jesus." There was nothing that any of our parents could have done to prevent us from inheriting Adam's sinful nature. Some of us are not problem children and are generally well behaved. But mankind will always have natural instincts to lie, cheat, hate, and do other sinful, evil acts. Some of us have more self-control than others. Yet we may fall short when no one is watching or there are no obvious consequences to our sin.

Is it fair that by Adam's act of sin you should be a sinner who needs to be saved from an eternity in hell? Well, God is awesome! Our Lord is forgiving and always willing to save us by his mercy and grace. Through one man, Christ Jesus, we receive an abundance of grace and the gift of righteousness that delivers us to eternal life in heaven (Romans 5:15, 19).

Jesus is the way to forgiveness for all the bad things you thought you got away with, all the times you intentionally hurt others, and all the bad things you said. If you wait until it's too late, you will have to pay a price that you cannot afford. Be very clear that eternal hell does mean forever! Will you answer the call of salvation so that you will be saved?

Lesson 1.1 Review

Multiple Choice

1. "_____ have sinned and fall short of the glory of God" (Romans 3:23).
   A. None B. Criminals C. All D. Addicts
2. The term "Adamic nature" means that Adam has passed this to all of mankind (Romans 5:12, 19).
   A. Human nature B. Mother nature
   C. Godly nature D. Sinful nature
3. What is the only way for you to see and enter the kingdom of heaven? (John 3:3, 5).
   A. Be born again B. Stop smoking/drinking
   C. Go to church D. Stay out of jail

True/False

1. Children are born without a sinful nature (Romans 3:23; Job 14:1).
2. Another name for Jesus is Immanuel, meaning God with us (Matthew 1:23).

Fill in the Blank

1. Jesus' mother, Mary, was married to Joseph. But Mary gave birth to Jesus by the power of the _____ _____ (Matthew 1:18).
2. "For the wages of sin is _____, but the gift of God is eternal life in Christ Jesus" (Romans 6:23).
3. "By one man's _____ many were made sinners, so by the obedience of one shall many be made righteous" (Romans 5:19).

Check Yourself

- ✓ Have you disobeyed anyone at home or school without apologizing?
- ✓ Are you willing to apologize?
- ✓ What can you do to prevent it from happening again?

1.2 Grace of God

What is grace? Grace is undeserved or unearned favor that God offers to everyone free of charge. God grants favor to everyone who turns their life to him no matter how long they were a sinner or how badly they may have sinned. This includes you, my dear friend!

Confession

Whenever I broke the rules at home or at school, I knew I would be punished. I never liked to ask my parents to sign my progress reports from school when I was failing a class. My punishment ranged from a slap upside my head to one week of restriction to my room. But my parents loved me dearly. They usually cut my punishment short or gave me an IOU for the whipping I deserved. I remember being confined to my room for three hours, which seemed like forever.

I eased out of my room with a pitiful look on my face, and asked in a soft voice, "Can I watch TV?"

"No!" my parents shouted.

"Please—I'll be good."

My begging went on and on. Finally, my parents said, "Go ahead, boy. But be in bed by ten o'clock."

I thought I had all the game. If I got on my parents' nerves long enough, they usually lifted my punishment just so they could have peace and quiet. I giggled quietly while watching television. I thought that I got one over on my lame parents. I was well aware that my inattentiveness and lack of effort in class deserved punishment. However, my parents were much sharper than I gave them credit for. They gave me light punishments to show me mercy and grace. Sure, I was taught with tough love plenty of times, but most of the time, my parents were examples of forgiveness and second chances. Although I continued to abuse my privileges and take my parents for granted, I received their grace.

Today, God is offering you the same opportunity to accept his free gift of grace to save your soul from hell. One day, those second chances to correct your behavior will run out. If you are blessed, you will not die in sin, but your bad attitude and crafty ways may land you in juvenile hall or the hospital. Even worse, someone close to you may have to pay for your misconduct. God hates sin and did not intend for you to die a sinner. "The Lord is faithful to his promise of salvation. He is patient, not willing that any should perish in hell, but that all should come to repentance [turn from sin]" (2 Peter 3:9, brackets added).

Did you know that sin separates you from God? In order to remain close to God, you have to repent, confess your sins, and ask for forgiveness on a daily basis. "If we confess our sins, [God] is faithful and just to forgive us our sins, and to cleanse us from unrighteousness" (1 John 1:9). Jesus did not deserve to die for mankind. Nor did Jesus have to choose to lay his life down for you. How many people would you die for? Most of us probably would not even accept someone else's punishment, let alone die for them.

As a youth, I really did not understand the importance of Jesus dying on the cross for mankind and for me. All I know is that many of my mentors and teachers showed me a lot of favor, even when I did wrong. It was easier for me to look up to those I could see on a daily basis before giving Jesus all the credit. I now understand that Jesus will use anyone to show his mercy and grace. The power of the Holy Spirit is why we get away with so much wrong, or think we do. Understand that God protected you as a sinner so he could draw you in as a believer. If God only showed us mercy and grace after we turned from sin, most of us would die in sin. Some of us would have been imprisoned, and many of us would have spent our entire youth in punishment.

Let's try to fully understand how much love, power, and grace was in Jesus' choice to lay his life down for us. Imagine the people you dislike the most. Think about the things you do not like about those who enforce rules in your school, neighborhood, juvenile courts, or home. Try to remember everyone who treated you unfairly, discriminated against you, and disrespected you. And consider those bullies who are always rude to you and cause you pain or discomfort. Guess what? *Those bad people are the same persons Jesus willingly laid his life down for so they do not have to spend eternity in hell!* Jesus made that ultimate sacrifice in love. Everybody has an equal opportunity to turn his or her life around. You may not think some people deserve a second chance, but there is also someone who thinks you do not deserve mercy and grace either.

> "For God so loved the world that he gave his only begotten son, that whoever believes in him should not perish, but have everlasting life" (John 3:16).

As a teenager, I did so much wrong I assumed God would never forgive me. I thought Christians were good people who never did anything wrong or never experienced the same challenges and obstacles I had to deal with. In my mind, I came from the poorest projects and lived in the roughest neighborhood with the toughest gangs. I assumed nobody could understand how hard I had to be to walk the streets I grew up on. I figured that once I cleaned up my act and straightened out my life, I would turn to God.

DJ, my youth mentor, once asked me an important question. "Do sick or injured persons heal themselves before they go to the hospital?"

I scratched my head, thinking it was a ridiculous question. DJ explained that I could never straighten out my own life. *God calls us to salvation while we are filthy from a disobedient lifestyle.* We may limp from pride or a broken heart of bitterness. Some of us need a face-lift from that angry mean-mug we wear all day.

First, we must turn to God, and then the healing process begins. Change may not come overnight, but *admitting your faults and seeking correction is the first step toward true change.* I told God I had a problem with following directions and admitted that I loved crime. Yes, God knows all and sees all. So when we admit our faults, it's not about informing God of something new. Confessing our sins proves that we are willing to make a positive change.

Every time you refuse to smoke, drink, or cuss you gain the victory. Most of your desires will not instantly go away, but as you stay in constant prayer and surround yourself with positive people, it gets easier to maintain your improved lifestyle. Over time, you will begin to dislike your old habits. When you witness others doing what you now refuse to do, you see how ugly those habits are. Cigarettes smell bad once you quit. Being drunk or high is not cool and is silly once you sober up. Skipping school is boring once you cut out all the nonsense and resist peer pressure. When you have a change of heart, it is impossible to criticize others without considering how you would feel to be teased, insulted, or disrespected.

*The greatest thing about salvation is that you do **not** have to work for it!* Do not talk yourself out of accepting Jesus into your life because you have not done enough good deeds. "For by grace are you saved through faith; and not of yourselves: it is a gift of God: Not of works, lest any man should boast" (Ephesians 2:8-9). Salvation is *free*!

Imagine if God said we had to work to be saved. Let's think about it. What if we had to read the entire Bible to receive salvation? Well, illiterate people could not be saved. What if we had to knock on doors and preach the gospel to be saved? Those who cannot walk would be left out. What if we had to donate so much money to the church to be saved? Then poor people would be left to die in hell. My point is that we do *not* work to be saved. We do good works and exhibit good behavior because we *are* saved! The difference is that when you wake up and realize that Christ delivered you from sin, you want to help other lost souls discover the goodness of God that you found. Every time you testify about the unhealthy, violent, or rebellious lifestyle that Christ empowered you to turn away from, you give hope to those who are headed down those same paths of destruction.

God poured out his grace to the adults in my life, and they passed that same undeserved favor to me. And now I'm passing it to you by directing you to Jesus. One day, you will look back and be thankful that you accepted the greatest gift of all. You know the truth. Do not run from your higher calling. Think about those times you made bad decisions and then looked back, wishing you would have made better choices. If you were like me—tricked into believing that bullying, rebellion, crime, and selfishness were your only options—now is the time to accept true change.

"God will have all men to be saved, and come into the knowledge of truth. For there is one God and one mediator between men and God, the man Christ Jesus" (1 Timothy 2:4-5). Do not allow others to discourage you from turning to Jesus. But most of all, do not allow yourself to hinder the blessings God has for you. Think about your dreams and goals. All you have to do is "seek first the kingdom of God and his righteousness, and all these things will be added to you" (Matthew 6:33).

Lesson 1.2 Review

Multiple Choice

1. "God so loved the world that he gave his one and only son (Jesus), that whoever _____ him shall not perish but have eternal life" (John 3:16).
   A. Work for   B. Believes in   C. Looks like
   D. Shouts about
2. What is God's grace?
   A. Favor you deserve   B. Blessings you earn
   C. Riches you want   D. Favor you don't deserve

True/False

1. God knows all so you do not have to confess your sins for forgiveness (1 John 1:9).
2. It's okay to boast about how much you worked to be saved (Ephesians 2:8-9).

Fill in the Blank

1. For by _____ are you saved through faith; and not of yourselves: it is the gift of God; Not works lest any man should boast" (Ephesians 2:8-9).

Check Yourself

✓ Have you ever received something that you know you did not deserve?
✓ What can you do to show a teacher or parent that you appreciate him or her?

1.3 My Choice of Salvation

When I was in ninth grade, I always procrastinated (put things off) when it came to obeying my parents. I was told to iron my clothes and take my bath at night. But why interrupt talking on the phone or watching television? I only needed a few minutes to get ready for school the next morning. I had it all figured out. All I had to do was wake up twenty minutes earlier than usual. However, I often stayed awake later than I was supposed to. Instead, my eyes stretched open to the sound of my mom's annoying voice. "Boy, you better be ready in five minutes!"

My laziness normally caused me to have to go to school in a wrinkled shirt. I regretted not being prepared in advance. In school, I always procrastinated when it came to completing assignments that were not due for weeks. I thought only nerds did homework in advance.

I found out the hard way when I refused to get my research paper done ahead of time in American Literature class. I was assigned to read *One Flew Over the Cuckoo's Nest.* I assumed the book was as dumb as its title, so I planned to read fifty pages a day. But, I also planned to hang out with my friends every day. I eventually skimmed the book and handed in my five-hundred-word report, and my teacher congratulated me for handing my assignment in on time. A few days later, when she returned the reports, my paper had so many red marks that it was obvious I neglected to proofread my work. My halfhearted effort should have gotten me an F, but my teacher was merciful enough to take into account that I had perfect attendance. Instead, I received a C—that I knew I did not deserve.

No matter how severe the consequences for procrastination were I never seemed to learn my lesson. At least not until my grandmother refused to give me money to buy a Bomb Pop from the ice cream truck. I stormed out of the apartment to hang with my friends. My grandmother spoiled me so much I could not accept no for an answer, and I barely spoke to her for two days. When I realized I was wrong, I planned to apologize when I came in from school, but it was too late.

The next time I saw my grandmother, her eyes were a dingy yellow. She was diagnosed with Hepatitis B, and the disease proved to be fatal. She whispered a few words of encouragement to me as she laid on her deathbed, but my grief was mostly due to the harsh reality that she would no longer be able to provide for me. I was so selfish I never thought to apologize for my bad attitude over the past few days. When my ill grandmother closed her eyes for the last time, I realized I had procrastinated in giving my apology for too long. My lack of consideration and selfishness can never be taken back. The missed opportunity was a heavy burden that I carried around for years.

Today, the only thing that could be worse than my procrastination as a youth would be to put off offering a call of salvation to adolescents. I fully understand that the possibility of *dying in sin is very real!* Do not find out that eternal hell is real after it's too late (John 3:18). What must you do to be saved?

> Confess with your mouth the Lord Jesus, and believe in your heart that God raised him from the dead, you shall be saved. With the heart man believes unto righteousness; and with the mouth confession is made to salvation . . . whoever shall call on the name of the Lord Jesus shall be saved (Romans 10:9-10).

My young brothers and sisters, tomorrow is not promised. Life comes with death, and we can be dead before receiving another chance to do the right thing. James 4:14 reminds us of how quickly life vanishes away. If you died today, would you go to heaven? How do you know? Jesus said, "I stand at the door and knock. If anyone hears my voice and opens the door, I will come into him" (Revelation 3:20). This Scripture is a metaphor, meaning that Jesus wants to come into your heart. Let Jesus into your life so he can save you from sin. Through your belief in Jesus, you can be blessed with an abundance of undeserved favor. All of your sins will be forgotten by God.

No one is perfect. King David was God's chosen leader of Israel, yet he repeatedly sinned and made mistakes. Why? David was a youth, just like you (1 Samuel 17:33). Even though he was young and not so perfect, God proclaimed that David was a man after God's own heart (Acts 13:22). Let's read King David's confession as he prayed to be saved from sin. "Remember not the sins of my youth, nor my transgressions: according to your mercy remember me for your goodness sake, O Lord" (Psalm 25:7).

Today, you can turn from your bad habits. God will only remember that you accepted Jesus. "[Jesus said] I am the way, the truth, and the life; no one comes to [God] the Father except through me" (John 14:6). The Lord constantly reminds us of how forgiving he is. "I will be merciful to their unrighteousness, and their sins and iniquities I will remember no more" (Hebrews 8:12). If you are willing to accept your call to salvation, read the following prayer to receive God's greatest gift: eternal life.

> Dear Heavenly Father, I thank you for inviting me into your Christian family. I am a sinner, and I do not deserve so much of your grace. But you said in your word that once I confess with my heart that Jesus is Lord and believe with all my heart that Jesus died to cleanse me of sin and that you raised Jesus from the dead, I will be saved. Please forgive me of my sins. Give me the strength and love to forgive those who have sinned against me. Come into my heart. Fill me with your Holy Spirit. Transform my mind, will, and emotions into the child of God that you want me to be. In Jesus' name I pray. Amen.

Congratulations, and welcome to the family of Christ Jesus! Today you have made the most courageous decision of your life. You have officially been born again. Your next step is to be baptized (Acts 2:38-39). If you have a church home, allow your pastor to perform your baptism ceremony. I suggest you attend at least one class to learn more about baptism. If you do not have a church home, you need a pastor to be your shepherd that offers a Bible teaching ministry as a covering to protect you from spiritual wickedness and sin that will always tempt you.

Baptism is an act of obedience after you have given your life to Christ. When your pastor lays you under the water, it is symbolic of you being buried with Christ. When your pastor lifts you out of the water, it symbolizes that you have been cleansed by the blood of Jesus and raised with Christ (Romans 6:1-6).

I pray that you allow men and women of God to teach you how to read the Bible and to be more like Christ. Your spiritual growth increases as you build a personal relationship with God. Pray daily. Find time to be alone and talk to God about your problems. Ask for wisdom and instructions about how to stay on the right path. You may have to end some friendships; avoid places that cause you to desire your old ways. Take your new way of life one day at a time. "If any man be in Christ, he is a new creature: old things are passed away, behold, all things are become new" (2 Corinthians 5:17).

Lesson 1.3 Review

Multiple Choice

1. Tomorrow is not promised. What should we say to show God appreciation and respect if he would allow our future plans to happen? (James 4:14)
   A. Hope   B. Cross my fingers
   C. I control my own future   D. Lord willing
2. Jesus said, "I stand at the door and knock. If anyone _____ and opens the door, I will come into him" (Revelation 3:20).
   A. Hears my voice   B. Is not home
   C. Ignores me   D. Hates to get up
3. No one comes to God the Father except through _____ (John 14:6).
   A. Death   B. Heaven   C. Jehovah   D. Jesus

True/False

1. Jesus says, "I knock at the door, if you open the door, I will come into you" (Revelation 3:20). This Scripture is a metaphor, meaning that Jesus wants you to let him into your heart so he can save you from sin.
2. God is so merciful that he will *not* remember our sins if we ask him for forgiveness (Hebrews 8:12).

Fill in the Blank

1. Confess with your mouth the Lord Jesus, and _____ in your heart that God raised him from the dead, you shall be saved" (Romans 10:9-10).
2. "Remember not the _____ of my youth, nor my transgressions: according to your mercy remember me for your goodness sake, O LORD" (Psalm 25:7).

3. "If any man be in _____, he is a new creature: old things are passed away, behold, all things are become new" (2 Corinthians 5:17).

Check Yourself

- ✓ Are you saved?
- ✓ If not, are you willing to give your life to Christ today?
- ✓ Now that you are saved, name one bad habit you need to break.

CHAPTER 2

BUILDING YOUR FAITH

In middle school, one of my classmates was named Gary. He was well behaved, outspoken, and a consistent Principal's Honor Roll student. Gary was always the first to raise his hand or volunteer. He always accepted the challenge to solve math problems in front of the class. I was not sure if Gary thought he was better than the rest of us or just hoped he could outperform the class.

Halfway through the school year, I began to realize that I was better than Gary in two areas: spelling and shooting free throws. But if any student wanted to know how to spell a word, he or she asked Gary. When coach needed a player to shoot technical free throws in a basketball game, Gary was his first choice. I did not understand back then that the major difference between Gary and me was that Gary loved to exercise his faith while I was afraid to fail in front of others.

What exactly is faith? Hebrews 11:1 says, "Faith is the substance of things hoped for, the evidence of things not seen." So what's the difference between hope and faith? Hope is a sincere expectation for good, but the end result may be out of your control. "I hope that my dad does not get laid off from his job." "I hope that my favorite team wins." Sometimes we hope for things we may never achieve or that may take too long for us to obtain. For instance, we hope for salvation (Romans 8:24-25). It's a struggle to constantly obey and do what's right according to God while not knowing how long it will be before Christ returns to save mankind. Through patience, obedience, and self-control, we claim our victory over death and hell.

Hope can also be when a person wants or wishes for something but does nothing to obtain it. Let's say you hope to pass your exam, but you did not take notes. You did not study. Your hope of passing may be the hope of guessing correctly. You do not want to drag through school hoping to do well. *It takes faith to graduate.* So how do you turn your hope into faith? To better understand, let's really get to know what faith is.

Faith means that there is substance to what you hope for. For example, you have faith that you will graduate high school. Sure, there are things beyond your control that can prevent you from graduating. However, you express your faith by having perfect attendance in school. You ask questions and get tutoring when you do not understand. You go to school with a positive attitude instead of complaining.

Your faith begins to materialize as you put forth your best effort to obtain what you hope for. Oftentimes, your faith builds as God grants you favor. Think about the blessings you received or the troubles you avoided that could not be explained. *God will help build your faith by giving you things you do not deserve or did not expect.* Oftentimes, you may not recognize the work of God, take the credit yourself, or give others the credit when God simply used them to be a blessing to you.

Faith is defined by your level of trust and belief. Your behavior is your trust/belief in action. For example, you can never claim to have faith and believe in your ability to graduate while your behavior proves that you are lazy and unwilling to put forth your best effort to pass. Faith without works is dead (James 2:17). *Your faith should be in God.* You must respect and obey the authority God has placed in your life, such as parents, teachers, police, church, and community leaders. "Obey them that have the rule over you, and submit yourselves: for they watch for your souls, as they must give account, that they may do it with joy, and not with grief: for that is unprofitable for you" (Hebrews 13:17).

It is *important for you to be active in a church home.* You along with everyone else need God's covering through elders who are accountable for your spiritual development. We all need godly advice to succeed as believers in Christ. The most difficult thing for me to accept as a youth in church was discipline. *Discipline is enforced obedience.* This gives you a sense of responsibility to be accountable for your own actions. Blaming others, making excuses, or doubting your abilities is unacceptable with God on your side. Faith consists of your learning to trust that God will put people in your life who are equipped to teach and raise you to maturity. However, rebellion does not lead to success. *When you disobey authority, you are actually disobedient to God.* Teachers enforce obedience to ensure that you live up to your full potential and strive for the best God has for you.

Remember, teachers have an authority to report to as well. No teacher is proud to have a *flunkee* in class, and no parent wants to brag about a rebellious child. Let's assume that the adults in your life are mean and difficult to get along with. Why should you obey them? "Do all things without murmurings and disputings. That you may be blameless and harmless, the sons of God, without rebuke, in the midst of a crooked and perverse nation, among whom you shine as lights in the world" (Philippians 2:14-15).

You may have teachers who cannot tolerate your performance, behavior, or unique personality. If so, that *does not give you a right to be disrespectful* and to lash out. Simply because your school is not properly equipped to teach you does not provide an excuse for you to cut class or drop out. God commands you to shine as a light in the midst of a black-hearted nation. You may not like your teacher, but that is no reason to disregard your teacher's advice. Sure, having faith in a bad teacher may lead to failure. But your faith in God will enable you to get proper tutoring and to take the initiative to learn under the worst conditions (1 Corinthians 2:5).

Understand that your witness as a child of God is at stake all the time. Others watch you, waiting to see you act just like the sinners. Some students may not believe you are a child of God until they witness you shining in dark situations. Even *as a youth, you have the power to draw in unbelievers to Christ's family* by how well you deal with rejection, misfortune, and unfairness. It is your job as a Christian to *never give others an excuse to disobey or sin* just because you are doing it. Faith allows you to lead by example what believers are to do in word, conduct, and love (1 Timothy 4:12).

Faith without works is dead! Unless you act on your faith, you may never accomplish what you truly believe in. When you have absolutely no clue how you will succeed or overcome an obstacle, simply pray and believe in your heart that God will make a way. Think positively by expecting better things to come because God hears all your desires, troubles, and goals you pray about (1 John 5:14-15).

Moral Lesson

To better understand how to apply your faith as a born-again believer in Christ, let's review an earthly example. Pretend God has empowered someone to give you your dream ride. Maybe you received a Bentley, Mercedes, or Ferrari. You would likely thank that person over and over. You would show appreciation by taking good care of your ride. However, you must be careful that your faith is in God and not the car or the person who gave you the free gift. The difference is, instead of praising the person who gave you the ride; you use your car to benefit others. It would be useless to leave your high-end automobile in the garage for your pleasure alone. You would let your friends ride in style with you. The more you see others sharing in your happiness; your faith grows because God has given you a special gift and because you have been chosen to receive a blessing that was not possible without God's help. Although the car does not define you, it is easier for you to meet others and have the opportunity to share your testimony of how God blessed you to afford the luxury ride. Trusting in God also means that you will not be so dependent on your new ride that if you lost it, you would also lose your sense of self-worth. Instead, you would have faith that God would provide another dream car, and until then, you are comfortable with whom you are.

The same principle works in the kingdom of God as a born-again believer. People notice that you are positive and hopeful in the worst of times. Your language does not consist of cussing and criticizing others. You are able to accept discipline and abide by rules even without adult supervision. You shine above all others with your attitude, willingness to help, and self-control. What God gives to new believers is much greater than a luxury car, money, or material things because those things can be lost, stolen, or destroyed, as *"car jackers"* and haters aim to take your possessions.

On the other hand, your priceless characteristics, such as joy and elevated self-esteem, rub off on others to help make their lives more worthy and less miserable. People look forward to your coming around, brightening their day and giving positive feedback or advice. Faith without works is dead! You do not have to shout in the middle of the street that you are a Christian. Simply allow your actions to speak for who you are and what you represent. You must be bigger than the gossip, fads/fashion, and in-crowd that are so popular in your environment. You become self-confident in whom God has created you to be. And no one can pull you down because you are defined by your ability to please God instead of your peers.

No one is perfect, but we can strive for perfection (Matthew 5:48). To improve your lifestyle, first, identify the areas of your life that are unacceptable to God. It's obvious that sin, rebellion, crime, and back talk has to be corrected. Have you considered helping others who may never repay you? Are you willing to forgive someone who you feel does not deserve forgiveness? Your body is the temple of God (1 Corinthians 6:19). Provide more care for your temple than you would for your dream ride or prized possession. "If any man defile the temple of God, him shall God destroy; for the temple of God is holy, which temple you are" (1 Corinthians 6:19).

Do not desecrate (destroy) God's house, i.e., your body, with filthy communication, excessive dating, and selfishness. Although you are young in the faith, there are some habits you should practice to help build your faith. Pray throughout the day, especially for matters beyond your control. Surround yourself with Christians and positive people. Ask questions when you read the Bible. Attend Bible study and church at least once a week. Do not aim to prove your faith in Jesus to the world; prove it to God! Remember that some people, including your friends, will be watching for you to sin, and then they will throw it in your face. As a new believer in Christ, beware of those who try to discredit your faith because you do not know very many Scriptures or biblical history. *It's okay to admit that you do not have all the answers, but be willing to learn* (2 Timothy 2:15-16, 23).

No matter how bad you have been or how much you have heard that you cannot change, I believe that you can succeed. As a believer in Jesus, you should show confidence about being saved. *God uses the least expected people to do great things.* Mary, the mother of Jesus, was a poor, young virgin. Paul, the apostle who wrote thirteen books of the New Testament, once persecuted Christians. Do not let others' doubt rub off on you. *Jesus was doubted by some of his own people* because of who his parents were. Many did not believe Jesus was good enough to perform miracles from God because of his family background (Matthew 13:54-58). Growing up in crime-infested, rundown housing projects or attending schools with higher dropout rates may cause people to misjudge you. If you believe you will remain at the bottom more than you trust in the miracle-working power of God, you may miss your blessing.

"Let no [one] despise [discredit] your youth, but be an example of the believers in word, conversation [conduct], charity [love], spirit, faith, purity" (1 Timothy 4:12, brackets added). The apostle Paul gave young Timothy this advice as he prepared to do God's work. I encourage you to be an example of godliness to believers and your peers. Do not allow anyone to discourage you if they look down on you because of your youth.

Have you ever corrected an adult or told them the appropriate way to do something only to be ignored? The same lack of consideration may occur as you become an example of godliness. Some will assume you are part of the problem and not the solution to your more violent, rebellious, young generation. The Scriptures confirm that if you wholeheartedly live by the Word of God, you can have more understanding than some teachers and elders (Psalm 119:99-100). *Believe it, and God will help you achieve it!*

2.1 Hearing the Word of God

The healthiest way to build your faith is to hear the Word of God (Romans 10:17). Your friends, parents, and teachers may not always speak or perform what is good according to God's Word. It is more difficult to build your faith if you are not hearing the Word of God throughout your daily routine. You do not have to hear preaching all day long, but those you spend most of your time with should minister to you by providing positive reinforcement, a sense of direction, conflict resolution, and correction. As a babe in Christ, you need to be fed spiritual nourishment, which is the Word of God. A malnourished or starving Christian is one that eats junk food, such as profanity, backbiting, hearsay, criticism, or doubt.

In my youth, none of my friends quoted the Bible, and many adults in my neighborhood openly used drugs, profanity, and violence. So how can youth in negative environments build their faith in Jesus when no one is speaking the Word of God? Actually, *in the worst situations, God is speaking to us most.* As born-again believers and children of God, the Holy Spirit is speaking to us even when we are alone. God's voice comes in the form of our thoughts, advising us what to do and what not to do. Positive self-talk is our navigation system from the Holy Spirit telling us where to go. The voice in your head that tells you not to skip school or to stay away from students pressuring you to do drugs is the voice of God guiding you toward what's best for you.

The Holy Spirit speaking within you may sound like the voice of those who feed you healthy, godly advice. I'm sure you have been in a position to make a bad choice when suddenly you recalled your parents or teachers warning you about the harmful consequences. And then you had the opportunity to correct your own behavior. Oftentimes, youth will choose to make the bad decision, hoping to not get caught or pay the penalty for misbehaving. Even the sound of a stranger's voice will stick with you, especially when his or her advice is important to your own personal bad experiences. The different voices of the persons God uses to speak to you will repeat in your head, especially when you are threatened by peer pressure, temptation, or danger.

*You are **not** too young to hear the voice of God.* Your goal is to master recognizing and responding to the voice of God that speaks directly to you or through others. As a child, the prophet Samuel was anointed to be God's minister. Samuel had a mentor named Eli, who helped him recognize the voice of God when Samuel was young (1 Samuel 3:1-10). At first, young Samuel was unsure of who he heard when God spoke to him, as he was too immature to understand that God will speak directly to a child. Young Christians like yourself will build your faith by believing that God is willing and able to speak to you. You must *expect to hear a word from God.*

You should know that *God also uses youths to deliver messages to save others.* I'm sure you have warned your parents or other adults to avoid doing something harmful and unwise. You may even have advised adults of what they *should* be doing. The Lord speaks to you every time that voice inside reminds you not to break the rules, motivates you to voluntarily show kindness, encourages you to be responsible when alone, and teaches you morals that adults may not have taught you.

To overcome being surrounded by negative influences or lacking adult supervision, listen to the voice of God that replays in your head. The gospel singers Mary, Mary performed the perfect song, "God in Me." *Being a minister (servant) of God has no age limit!* Serving God is not like acquiring a driver's license or being old enough to enlist in the military. *You can minister the Word of God to others right now.* How, you ask? Well, godliness does not mean you have to know Bible passages, be an elder in the church, or even be an adult. Simply advise others not to cuss. Encourage students to attend school. Invite a friend to church. Have self-control to be a positive influence to the out-of-control youngsters. These are effective ways of being a servant of God that you are very capable of performing right now. Let's review more examples of youth being used in mighty ways by God.

Samson was physically one of the mightiest men of God and was a child when God anointed (blessed) him to do God's work (Judges 13:24-25). King David was anointed to rule over Israel as a boy (1 Samuel 16:12-13). As a youth, David also accepted the challenge to conquer Goliath (1 Samuel 17:32-33). And did you know that Jesus was only twelve years old when he grew strong in spirit and wisdom? He was in the temple listening to his teachers and asking them questions (Luke 2:40-47).

God's Word holds true today as it did thousands of years ago and will remain true forever. *God is with you always. The more you recognize that God is speaking directly to you, the stronger your faith will become.* To consistently hear God's voice, pay close attention to the message and not the messenger. For example, do not disregard godly advice when it comes from a drug addict who's teaching you how to avoid falling into the trap he or she is in. Listen to the hustler when he warns you that life in prison is given to youth more frequently. No matter how ungodly your parents or family members may be, they can still teach you what *not* to do. Stop, listen, and learn. Hear how the Holy Spirit is guiding and teaching you, and then your faith will grow.

Lesson 2.1 Review

Multiple Choice

1. "_____ is the substance of things hoped for, the evidence of things not seen" (Hebrews 11:1).
   A. A wish   B. A prayer   C. Magic   D. Faith
2. Who should you put your faith into? (1 Corinthians 2:5)
   A. The power of God   B. The hands of your parents
   C. Teachers   D. Preachers
3. What does it mean to desecrate or defile your body? (1 Corinthians 3:17)
   A. Build   B. Destroy   C. Exercise   D. Wash
4. As a child, what did the prophet Samuel hear? (1 Samuel 3:1-10)
   A. Murderers   B. Devils   C. God's voice
   D. Dead people
5. This mighty man of God was a boy when God chose him to judge (rule) the kingdom of Israel (Judges 13:24-25).
   A. Goliath   B. Abraham   C. Samson   D. Adam

True/False

1. Your body is the temple of God (1 Corinthians 6:19).
2. David was a boy when he was anointed (chosen/blessed) to be king of Israel (1 Samuel 16:12-13).

Fill in the Blank

1. "Faith without _____ is dead" (James 2:17, 26).
2. "_____ comes by hearing, and hearing by the word of God" (Romans 10:17).
3. "You are the _____ of God, and the Spirit of God dwells (lives) in you" (1 Corinthians 3:16).

Check Yourself

- ✓ Who or what do you listen to the most?
- ✓ Have you heard a gospel song or preaching lately?
- ✓ Name someone or something you should not be listening to because it is negative or explicit?

2.2 Receiving the Word of God

After I accepted the call to salvation, I discovered that applying God's wisdom and instructions to my life was difficult. There were bad habits that I immediately turned from, but most of my wrongdoings were hard to break. By my senior year in high school, my heart rejected most advice, and I disliked anyone who told me what to do. Adults only wanted me to be more Christ-like. I spent nearly twenty years rejecting God's Word before I received it. For you to fully understand how to receive the Word of God, let's review the parable of the sower.

What is a parable? *A parable is a story that illustrates and teaches a moral lesson.* Jesus spoke in parables, using an earthly description to deliver a heavenly message. Parables usually consist of analogies, similes, or metaphors. Why did Jesus speak in parables? He spoke in parables to reveal knowledge and wisdom to born-again believers and to those seeking the truth. *And to conceal heavenly things from sinners or those who reject the truth.* Let's review the metaphors Jesus uses in the parable of the sower (Matthew 13:1-23).

What is a sower? *A sower is one who plants or scatters seed in a garden, field, etc.* The phrase "You reap what you sow" means that whatever kind of seed you plant (sow) is the exact same fruit/plant you will harvest or gather in (reap). In other words, you get what you deserve! In the same manner that apple seeds bring forth apples, good deeds to others bring good things back to you. If you sow sin, you will reap death and condemnation to hell. By sowing forgiveness to others, you reap forgiveness from God.

In the parable of the sower, Jesus uses "<u>seed</u>" as a metaphor for the Word of God, and "sower" is a metaphor for Jesus, who plants the Word of God into the soil (our heart). Jesus uses four different metaphoric phrases to express the "soil" (heart) receiving or rejecting the Word of God. The moral lesson Jesus reveals to us is that the Word of God is true and never fails (Isaiah 55:11). Instead, it's our heart's misplaced desires and wrong intentions that prevent us from receiving the Word of God. Now, let's analyze the four metaphoric phrases Jesus uses.

1. "And when he sowed, some seeds fell by the wayside, and the fowls [birds] came and devoured them up" (Matthew 13:4). Jesus is referring to a person choosing to *not* receive the Word of God in his heart. The word (seed) is wasted as it scatters by the wayside. Have you heard the cliché, "Going in one ear and out the other"? *A key reason you cannot grow spiritually and build your faith is that you reject God's Word.* You may refuse to listen to godly advice, or you may not obey. The Word of God is wasted by ignoring advice, not following instructions, or justifying doing it "my way," which usually leads to trouble.

I had such little faith as a teen. I did not believe an inner city youth had a fair opportunity to become a doctor, lawyer, or President of the United States. Therefore, I could not receive the word, "I can do all things through Christ Jesus which strengthens me," (Philippians 4:13). I only allowed the Scripture to pertain to my accomplishing goals within reach at that time, such as making honor roll, winning a wrestling match, and staying off drugs. Unlike the younger generation of today, I did not have many examples of success that were a reflection of my race or cultural background. Today there are wealthy people who came from unfavorable and unlikely situations to be successful, e.g., P. Diddy, music mogul; Barack Obama, President of the United States; Oprah Winfrey, billionaire; and Robert Johnson, BET founder. I did not personally know any doctors, lawyers, or politicians. I heard of Jesse Jackson, Johnny Cochran, Maxine Waters, and Bill Cosby. But those careers represented hopes and dreams I could never have. Now there are real examples of children who planted seeds and became millionaires: Bow Wow, rapper; Nick Cannon, Miley Cyrus, and Raven Simone, Nickelodeon stars; and the Olsen twins, retailers.

*Do **not** allow race, gender, finances, or anything kill your faith. Everyone* faces some degree of difficulty to be successful. As a youth, *set smaller goals that lead toward your long-term plan of success.* Right now, stay in school. Practice self-discipline. Deny yourself those pleasures that lead to drug addiction, obesity, injury, teen pregnancy, crime, bullying, and death. Remember: *Discipline is enforced obedience.* Make your own decision to clean your room and obey curfew. Finish your homework so your parents do not have to always enforce the rules. The Word of God teaches us that it is right for children to obey their parents, so teens should honor their mother and father (Ephesians 6:1-3). Will you receive this word from God?

2. "Some [seeds] fell on stony places, where they had not much earth: they sprung up . . . And when the sun was up, they were scorched, and because they had not much root they withered away" (Matthew 13:5-6, brackets added). When Jesus says the stony places had not much earth, he means the soil was not deep enough. Just beneath the topsoil were rocks or a hard surface that prevented the roots of a budding seed from stabilizing the plant. Roots nourish the plant. Roots also hydrate the plant and prevent the plant from being easily plucked up. *Another reason you cannot build your faith and grow spiritually is that you are not rooted and grounded in the Word of God.* You may have received the Word of God, but it is easily plucked up when trouble strikes, e.g., like when you argue with students, impress your peers, take advantage of the weak, date teens, or rebel against adults. You may generally be a great kid, but as soon as you do not get your way or get your feelings hurt, you are likely to forget about God and lash out in disrespect.

Moral Lesson

In ninth grade, I broke my curfew by going to a late-night party without asking permission. I did it on purpose to prove to my friends that I was not a "lame" or a "square." I knew I would be punished, but it seemed worth the risk. My dad showed up. I was embarrassed in front of my classmates, so I decided to defend my reputation. My father had to show me tough love and discipline, but I responded with rebellion. My bitterness, anger, and loud talking were the exact opposite of how the Word of God teaches us to act (Ephesians 4:31). When I felt humiliated in front of my classmates, it was very easy for me to forget about obeying my father because the Word of God was not rooted in my heart. When Dad called my name, I was bitter because the students laughed at me and there was nothing I could do about it. I refused to be escorted out of the party, so Dad pulled me by the arm. I was angry I as pleaded my case to stay and have fun. Dad told me to lower my voice. I yelled, "I'm not talking loud!" Dad then used more force to drag me out of the party. Then I dropped the bomb. "I hate you!"

My intention was to embarrass my dad as much as I was. The difference was that Dad was in line with the Word of God by disciplining me, and I was in disobedience (Hebrews 12:6-7). I got the worst whipping of my life, and I never disrespected my dad again.

Parents enforce obedience on children only because they love them and so does God. Youth have to learn the discipline of obedience, responsibility, and accountability for their actions. Unfortunately, many teens have to learn the hard way. Parents would be considered unfit or wrong if they allowed teenagers to repeat the same mistakes that could cause harm to themselves or others. *Without consequences and punishment, most teens would never obey.*

Remember, as a youth most of your decisions are based on emotions, pride, reputation, and image. You lack the experience to make informed decisions. *God uses parents and other adults to teach you lessons that you have not lived long enough to fully understand.* When you accept discipline and instruction, your faith builds because you know that God will not allow you to waste your talents, miss opportunities, or head in the wrong direction. Sometimes you have to be grounded to your room in order to learn how to be rooted and grounded in the Word of God.

3. "Some [seeds] fell among thorns; and the thorns sprung up, and choked them out" (Matthew 13:7). The thorns represent misbehavior and bad habits or selfishness and sinful intentions. *The third reason you cannot grow spiritually and build your faith is due to the hidden motives within your heart that choke out the Word of God.* As a teenager, pride hindered my moral and spiritual growth. I grew up in the gangbanging era that promoted "stop snitching" campaigns, much like today. The code of silence was so strong that I did not want to speak out against wrong. And anybody who told when I misbehaved was labeled a rat or snitch. The Word of God cannot be applied with the same method as G-Codes, which are rules of thugs. God's laws are to be shouted on the mountaintops and used with mercy and grace.

When we apply God's pure Word to our unhealthy lifestyle, it's the same as the seeds that fell among thorns mentioned in the parable of the sower. For example, it does you no good to tell the truth only when it's convenient or when there are no obvious consequences for being honest about what you did wrong. Teens are not the only ones who lie. Many God-fearing adults, including myself, have excused telling a lie. However, we adults are quick to tell the whole truth when gossiping behind someone's back. *The Word of God is not a light switch that can be turned on to reveal someone else's dirty secrets but turned off to conceal your own faults.* You are not alone. Everyone struggles with turning from old habits and blocking out negative thinking in order to live by the Word of God.

My advice to you is to identify your intentions, desires, or habits that hinder your lifestyle as a Christian. Pray that God empowers you to clear your heart and conscience of all things that will cause you to compromise (make excuses or change) the Word of God. Take me, for example. As a teen, I knew it was wrong to sell drugs, but I did it anyway because I claimed to have love in my heart and could be a blessing to people. I compromised what love truly is by giving bigger crack rocks to addicts. And I gave my friends drugs to sell because I "loved" to see them happy to get paid.

Anytime you compromise God's Word, it will come back to haunt you, for you reap what you sow! The same people that I "loved" to help went to jail and some of them told on me. In the end, we were all in juvenile hall, blaming each other. While I was locked in that tiny cell, I blamed God for allowing me to get locked up. But God's plan was to use incarceration to reveal that I did not have a good heart (Jeremiah 17:9).

Every time I suffered the consequences for my actions, I was uncertain if I was really saved. Sometimes my punishments were so bad I questioned if God really existed. "A double-minded man is unstable in all his ways" (James 1:8). Playing with the Devil and living for God will never allow your faith to build no matter how much of God's Word you receive. You cannot love God and hate people, including your enemies (Matthew 5:44). You cannot be at peace with God while warring with your siblings, parents, or classmates. Your religion is no good if you praise God with the same tongue used to curse others (James 1:26; 3:8-10). Before we continue to build on the Word of God, we may need to tear down the ways of the Devil.

4. "Other [seeds] fell into good ground, and brought forth fruit, some an hundred, some sixty, some thirty fold" (Matthew 13:8). In this final example, Jesus reveals that good ground is a healthy and pure heart that receives the Word of God. The fruit of your labor multiplies to benefit yourself and others. When you plant an apple seed, one apple does not grow. An apple *tree* grows. You can pick those apples and share with others for years. When you receive the Word of God, you are blessed to be a blessing to others.

So what is growing inside the new believer that can be shared with others? Let's review the fruit of the Spirit. "The fruit of the Spirit is love, joy, peace, longsuffering [patience], gentleness, goodness, faithfulness, meekness, temperance [self-control]" (Galatians 5:22-23, brackets added). Consider yourself a student learning how to consistently produce ripe spiritual fruit, and apply the same principles that help students succeed in school. Join a church and attend Bible study (2 Timothy 2:15). Have perfect attendance, take notes, ask questions, study on your own, and learn from the mistakes you make on each test. Your test may be to humble yourself when someone says something negative to or about you. Do not respond with criticism or bad words. Do your chores without having to be told. Be on your best behavior when no adults are around to supervise you.

To build your faith, you must prove that you trust and believe in Christ more than you believe in your own abilities or opportunities. For example, you may want to own a business, but perhaps you are not so great in mathematics. Maybe your family has no money to send you to college. You may not even know anyone who owns a business. But you do your best in school while researching how business owners operate and succeed. Go online and watch educational programs. There are even reality shows that portray behind-the-scenes footage of what it takes to run a business. Much of your free time should be geared toward studying the profession you want to master.

In order to be God's child and achieve the best God has to offer, you must also study how to live more Christ-like. Tune in to pastors on television. Watch BET's *Bobby Jones Gospel* and *Lift Every Voice*. You are in training at church, Sunday school, and Bible study. Be an active member by joining the youth choir and usher board. Your homework is to read the Bible at least once a day on your own time. Christian exams are held wherever you go: school, movies, the mall, sporting events, park, cruising, a friend's house, your own home, etc.

If your peers tease you because you are not living by the code of the streets or upholding a rep, your notes of how to pass the test are located in the Bible (Proverbs 29:23; 16:18). If others judge you because you speak properly, respectfully, and without nasty language, use the Bible references of James 1:26; 3:6. Do your research on all the hustlers and criminals who are dead or in prison. Your encyclopedia to prevent you from giving in to the temptation to make fast money is 1Timothy 6:9-10 and Matthew 7:13-14.

The Bible is not reserved only for adults, teachers, and wise people. The Word of God is also for ordinary young people like you! As God opens the eyes of your understanding, you begin to see your lifestyle, troubles, and hope of succeeding in those Bible stories. Recognize other believers in Christ and get to know them. Your Facebook and Twitter are those following Christ in your school, neighborhood, and home. Identify the sinners and troublemakers by the blogs coming out of their mouths. Log off and disconnect from people who will eventually bring you down (Proverbs 20:11; Romans 16:17).

Lesson 2.2 Review

Multiple Choice

1. Jesus spoke in _____, which are stories that use similes or metaphors to illustrate a moral lesson (Matthew 13:3).
   A. Riddles   B. Tongues   C. Parables   D. Morse code
2. In the parable of the sower, Jesus is the Sower. _____ is a metaphor for the Word of God (Matthew 13:20).
   A. Seed   B. Plant   C. Vine   D. Branch
3. In the parable of the sower, he that receives the "seed" in good ground is he that _____ and understands the Word of God (Matthew 13:23).
   A. Buries   B. Hears   C. Refuses   D. Gives
4. Whoever is _____ like a little child is the greatest in the kingdom of heaven (Matthew 18:4).
   A. Impatient   B. Curious   C. Innocent   D. Humble
5. _____ will cause destruction and failure (Proverbs 16:18).
   A. Poverty   B. Cheap clothes   C. Friendliness   D. Pride
6. The _____ causes a fire, sin, and can corrupt the whole body (James 3:5-6).
   A. Hair   B. Tongue   C. Bad breath   D. Body odor

True/False

1. In the parable of the sower, he that receives the "seed" among the "thorns" has heard God's Word, but his cares of the world and deceitfulness of riches chokes out the word (Matthew 13:22).
2. Jesus spoke in parables to reveal the mysteries of heaven to some and to conceal it from others (Matthew 13:11-12).
3. The Lord does not punish or whip those he loves (Hebrews 12:6-7).

Fill in the Blank

1. "I can do all things through _____ which strengthens me" (Philippians 4:13).
2. _____ to show yourself approved to God (2 Timothy 2:15).
3. Wide is the gate and broad is the way that leads to _____; many will take this path (Matthew 7:13).
4. Even a _____ is known by his doings, whether his work be pure and right (Proverbs 20:11).

Check Yourself

- ✓ Have you rejected good advice lately?
- ✓ Will you ignore good advice next time?
- ✓ What can you do to show your parent(s) or teacher(s) that you will now receive their good advice?

CHAPTER 3

WALKING IN REPENTANCE

As a teenager, I thought I knew all the tricks and schemes to compromise doing what is right. To compromise what's right simply means to make the excuse that there is no difference between right and wrong. The intentions of compromising righteousness may be to escape punishment, gain by deceit, or mislead someone to believe an act of unrighteousness has not been committed. I always compromised telling the truth by exaggerating the facts.

One day, my mother asked me, "Boy, did you eat up all the cookies?"

I knew I had eaten all but three of the cookies. However, I reasoned that it was okay to deny eating *all* the cookies because there were a few left in the bag. So I compromised the truth and was punished because exaggerating the truth, or deceiving, is the same as lying.

Now that you have repented (turned from sin) and given your life to Christ, you cannot compromise the truth. Let's better understand what repentance means. Repentance is a change of mind that brings about a change of action. You cannot have one without the other or else you have compromised repentance.

For example, when I was in juvenile hall, I repented from smoking cigarettes. There was a change of action because I had no access to cigarettes. But in my mind, I craved a smoke. I had not made up my mind to turn down a cigarette when I had the next opportunity to smoke. The same day that I was released, I immediately smoked the first available cigarette. Had I truly repented, I would have fought off the urge to smoke and would have avoided smokers and where they hung out.

Another example was when I was in college. I made up my mind to stop smoking marijuana. I knew that cigar paper caused cancer and that my grades were poor due to my short-term memory loss. I understood marijuana made my appetite inconsistent and noticed my mood swings when I could not get high. In my mind, I was convinced it was unhealthy to smoke, yet I continued my same behavior. I had not truly repented and still hung out with potheads, even though I suffered regret after smoking. Although I had the proper information to repent, I was just too weak mentally to repent and change my behavior.

> Present your bodies a living sacrifice, holy, acceptable to God, which is your reasonable service. And be not conformed to this world: but be transformed by the renewing of your mind that you may prove what is that good, acceptable, and perfect, will of God (Romans 12:1-2).

As a new believer in Jesus, your first reasonable service is to sacrifice your bad attitudes: being a smart aleck, throwing temper tantrums, using filthy language, bullying, and being rebellious. These bad habits have to be sacrificed because they must die with your old self. You were crucified with Christ and raised a new creation (Colossians 3:8-10).

Turning from sin is a process called sanctification that may not feel so good in certain areas of your life at first. Sanctification simply means to set yourself apart. For example, you may live in the projects or go to the worst school, but that is no excuse for you to act like those who are disrespectful, foul-mouthed, and destructive.

You may even have to interact with ungodly persons. But you sanctify yourself by being an example of Christ and displaying self-control (Philippians 2:15). For example, when you sit at the lunch table with sinners, you are sanctified when you pray for your food, are thankful instead of critical of the food, clean up after yourself, and leave as soon as you eat so others may sit down.

Sanctification does not always mean you can physically segregate yourself from sinners. Bad people are everywhere—home, school, and work, even the church. If a sinner attacks your faith or causes you to stumble, remove yourself. Do not get into a debate in an attempt to defend your faith. And know that when you hang around bad company others will judge you because you are a born-again believer. However, your job is to allow God to use you to save souls! Therefore, you will have to speak with sinners and tell them how God has improved your life. Sometimes your witness is more powerful by simply saying nothing and letting your actions speak for you.

For you to walk in true repentance, you must witness to unsaved or backslidden souls. Did you know that Jesus was wrongfully accused for befriending publicans and sinners? Jesus said, "Wisdom is justified of her children" (Matthew 11:19). Did you know that Matthew, the disciple Jesus chose, was previously a publican (tax collector) that was thought to be a sinner? (Matthew 9:9-10; Luke 5:27-32). Of course, you should not act like the sinners or justify their behavior. Instead, when you are in the presence of sinners, allow them to hear the call of salvation God has promised all mankind (2 Peter 3:9; James 5:20).

To walk in true repentance, you cannot be conformed to this world. To be conformed means to be shaped and molded by outside influences. In this case, do not allow unbelievers to shape and mold your character and conduct. You do not have to skip school, date, or hang out late because most of your peers are doing it. Prove yourself to God, not mankind! The true identity of a believer walking in repentance and following Christ is love (John 13:34-35). You need an ID to cash a check. You should also present your ID of love to walk a path that will get you into the kingdom of heaven.

Walking in repentance does not mean you cannot have fun. You do not have to be a party-pooper. Christianity was not intended for you to sit around bored. Go to the mall, go bowling, see a movie, go cruising, and tell jokes. But do it with your Christian family and friends who do not need drugs, alcohol, sexual perversion, or crime to have a great time. Walking in repentance is not done alone. You will discover a core circle of friends who are compatible with your personality. Many Christians like you are trying to find a child of God who also knows how to kick it. Put some pep in your step. Bring life and excitement when you come around. Smile. An upbeat personality is a magnet that attracts people with a sense of humor and an, outgoing personality.

I know what it's like to be so serious about God that you never express joy. I remember being in a room full of Christians, who were equally as sincere as me about repentance. We sat apart and gave one another a cold greeting. Newcomers looked in and then hurried away. Our attitudes were uninviting. Our dull conversation and stone faces could not draw anyone into the body of Christ. Christians should not continually look sad and be antisocial. We should be praising the Lord in happiness, love, thanksgiving, sharing, and unity to add to our church families (Acts 2:46-47).

3.1 Being God's Child

As a teen, my parents granted me freedom to make my own decisions in school, sports, and other extracurricular activities. They advised me to enroll in classes that best suited my career goals, hobbies, and personal interests and recommended I take courses that were challenging enough to build me up in areas I was weak in.

But no matter how much wisdom and knowledge I received, it was up to me to perform well. I had to be responsible enough to ask for help or clarification when necessary. I was fortunate to have forgiving parents who tolerated my shortcomings, but I received harsh punishment when my behavior was totally opposite of what I was taught. When I think back, there were many times my behavior did not reflect that I was a child of God.

I mistook my parents' kindness for weakness. I begged so much that my parents went against their better judgment to please me. But I was never satisfied. I abused their willingness to allow me to speak my mind and often argued or debated about their methods of discipline. I talked loud to get my point across when I was supposed to be obedient to instructions. I communicated with a lack of consideration as if my parents were my peers and gave no honor to their authority. I assumed I was smarter and more skilled than my parents. I thought I could run our household.

Learn from my mistakes. For you to be a child of God, you must submit to authority (Ephesians 6:1-3). Do not think that you are more talented or gifted than your parents. You have no right to challenge their authority. My parents often felt I betrayed their trust and disrespected their advice, and I did. Jesus feels the same disrespect when you are disobedient and rebellious. You have to be accountable for your own actions, as you cannot hide from God. Telling lies to get out of trouble only gets you into deeper sin. All you have to do is confess to God, who forgives all (1 John 1:9), and then tell your parents the truth and accept the consequences of your actions instead of lashing out as if they are provoking you with discipline. "No chastening [punishment] for the present seems to be joyous, but grievous [painful]: nevertheless afterwards it yields the peaceable fruit of righteousness to them which are exercised thereby" (Hebrews 12:11, brackets added).

Jesus said, "For whosoever shall do the will of my Father which is in heaven, the same is my brother, and sister, and mother" (Matthew 12:50). To be in Christ's family, we must obey. No matter how bad the circumstances appear, we have to trust in God's forgiveness. That means we ask for forgiveness as well as forgive others. Yes, it's scary to tell the truth when you have done wrong. You may not fear being physically hurt, but you are reluctant to reveal that you disobeyed, especially when you have been taught not to do so.

Why do you fear God or his authority working in others whenever you fall short?

> They shall be my people, and I will be their God: And I will give them one heart, one way, that they may fear me forever; for the good of them, and of their children after them, that I will not turn away from them, to do the good; but I will put my fear in their hearts, that they should not depart from me (Jeremiah 32:38-40).

God's will is for us to love him yet fear him enough to be totally dependent on him instead of turning our backs and running from discipline and instruction. Think of how scary it would be to leave home. How would you earn money? Where would you sleep? Who would care enough to give you advice to keep you out of trouble? To turn from God would be the same as running away from heaven, which is your eternal home. God promised to be your Father forever, no exceptions! He will never leave you. But you must choose to abide by the rules of living in God's house as his child.

Godly fear is intended to keep you obedient to God as he works through your guardians, parents, and those who help you stay on the right track. On the other hand, when you give the wrong person authority in your life, godly fear is also transferred. You no longer fear God and his saints. Instead, you fear leaving the gang, turning from crime, cutting loose friends who are a bad influence, and stopping the rebellion. Why? These things have become your gods.

When you choose to follow bad people and unhealthy lifestyles, you are making them your idols. They then have more influence over you than Jesus Christ.

Have you ever met a girl who was too scared to leave her abusive boyfriend? Do you know a person who is so conceited that he fears not having high-end fashions and material things? You may know someone who cares more about what others think of her. These people fear those that they have given authority over their lives to. Displaced authority is abused to keep you in a relational trap. Your friends should not be such a big influence that you dislike your parents. Your classmates should not have the power over you to cause you to fail just to be in the in-crowd. A child of God is more afraid of disobeying God and his authority than anyone else. Today is your opportunity to get out of those relational traps and turn to God! Which consequences do you want: lose your life in heaven forever or lose your so-called friends, who will only help you fall?

Godly fear is meant to bring you to sorrow for your sins, mistakes, and bad decisions. Anyone who does not feel a sense of conviction for his or her shortcomings is not a child of God. Believers in Christ feel bad and remorseful when we cause harm, even if our actions were accidental or unintentional. "Now I rejoice, not that you were made sorry, but that you sorrowed to repentance . . . Godly sorrow works repentance to salvation . . . but the sorrow of the world works death" (2 Corinthians 7:9-10).

We have all experienced worldly sorrow, which is when you are sorry simply because you got caught doing something wrong or you have apologized because someone forced you to. Worldly sorrow is asking for forgiveness and then intentionally repeating the same offense. It takes godly sorrow to walk in true repentance. You should feel ashamed of what you did wrong and be willing to go the extra mile to make amends or repair relationships you have torn down. You should also commit in your heart to never hurt another person, including yourself, in that manner again.

Godly sorrow allows you to realize that your faults caused much pain and affected more people than just you. As a child of God, you must seek forgiveness and repentance daily. And temptations are sure to come. You are too weak to fight off Satan, as you are not experienced enough to walk in repentance alone (2 John 4:4). Did you know that in your weakness Jesus' strength is made perfect (2 Corinthians 12:9)? How? When you are broken, you feel defeated and are empty of selfishness. Only then are you ready for Christ to guide you instead of rebelling and disobeying.

Imagine if you were locked up. You would pray and do anything that would set you free. If you were on fire, you would call on God and be willing to do anything to put out those hot flames. Well, Christ wants us to feel in need of his mercy and grace at all times, not just when we are at our weakest, most desperate points. Humble yourself. When you receive blessings, your first priority is to be thankful to God and share them with others. You should not be more concerned with boasting than you are willing to share. When you get chastised at home or school, accept that your actions warranted punishment. Stop blaming others for treating you unjustly or unfairly when in reality you were disobedient.

As a child of God, you can take control by learning self-control. If your parents fuss at you for not doing your chores, do not talk back. No matter how well-spoken you are, the fact remains that you did not do your chores. When you fail a class, you may have the best argument that the teacher picked on you or gave you tests with a higher degree of difficulty. However, it was your fault for not studying or taking notes. You should have communicated to your parents and school staff that you were having difficulty in class. Do not wait until you suffer consequences before you seek help or advice.

I believe that you have learned some valuable lessons that will help you walk in true repentance. But do you believe you can do better?

Lesson 3.1 Review

Multiple Choice

1. Be transformed by renewing your _____ to prove what is acceptable to God (Romans 12:2).
   A. Mind   B. Habits   C. Goals   D. License
2. Who should you obey first and foremost to be considered in Jesus' family? (Matthew 12:50).
   A. Mom   B. Dad   C. God the Father   D. Police
3. What leads us to repent (turn from) sin/crime? (2 Corinthians 7:9-10).
   A. Jail   B. Injury   C. Getting caught   D. Godly sorrow

True/False

1. Foolish questions lead to arguments and trouble (2 Timothy 2:23).
2. Only those who receive Jesus have the power to be sons/daughters of God (John 1:12).
3. God does not put godly fear in his children to prevent them from leaving Him (Jeremiah 32:38-40).

Fill in the Blank

1. "He that covers his _____ shall not prosper [succeed]: but whoever confesses and turns from them shall have mercy" (Proverbs 28:13).
2. Jesus said, "My grace is sufficient for you: My strength is made perfect in weakness" (2 Corinthians 12:9).
3. When you help a sinner convert to Christianity and turn from sin, you _____ a soul from death (James 5:20).

Check Yourself

- ✓ Do you believe that you are a child of God?
- ✓ Is there a person you hang with or a place you hang at that is ungodly?
- ✓ What area of your life or personality displays you as God's child?

3.2 Resisting Temptation

My mother used to say, "Boy, everything that looks good to you ain't good for you."

Mom usually said that when I begged for new Jordan sneakers or the latest high-dollar fashions. The problem with my expensive taste was that juvenile delinquents were stealing clothes right off kids' back. I found out the hard way that mom was right.

My flag football coach was a preacher. Every time coach saw us staring at girls, he said, "The lustful desire of the flesh causes bad judgment." Unfortunately, I did not understand what he meant. But the message became very clear when I caught a fever blister from kissing the "friendliest" girl on the block.

When I was a youth, my grandmother was like Jesus. She spoke the truth in riddles that I could never solve. Grandma said, "Pride will cause you more harm than good." Like the time my best friend dared me to jump my bike over an eight-foot ramp; I only did it because I was the runt of the crew. I still have the bruise on my forehead to prove I was not scared, though.

I experienced many dumb moments as a teenager. I cannot recall all the times my friends set me up for failure, injury, or humiliation. When I first became a Christian, I continued to pay for my choice to fall into temptation. I questioned God, "Why are you tempting me?" I have since learned that I was wrong to blame God (James 1:13-14). God tests us, but the Devil tempts us. Let's analyze the differences to better understand the obstacles meant to help us grow in faith and resist temptation versus the obstacles meant to cause doubt and lead us into temptation.

A test from God is used to prove your faithfulness, self-worth, abilities, and commitment. For example, let's say you want a pair of sneakers. Your friend invites you to work with him at McDonald's, but you really don't want to work there because your friends will laugh at you and the people you want to impress most will not respect you. And you will have to get dirty. If you feel this way, you are receiving a test from God that challenges you to put aside your pride and humble yourself. If you humble yourself and work an honest job, you get rewarded with a paycheck, build your sense of independence, and start establishing a work history for your future career.

Satan uses our desires to tempt us into sin, rebellion, crime, or disobedience. Using the same example, let's say you want a pair of sneakers. Your friend invites you to hustle with him, which you really enjoy because the money comes so fast and the people you want to impress most will look up to you. And you can show off while others are begging their parents for new gear. If you feel this way, the Devil is tempting you by taking advantage of your pride. If you give in to your pride, you risk going to jail, you could get robbed, and you lose the respect you would gain from making an honest living.

How would you bait a bear into a trap? You would not use veggies knowing that the bear likes meat. So you would lure the bear into the trap with beef or pork. A rabbit likes veggies, so carrots or lettuce would be enticing. The reason why you are unable to resist temptation is that you see the things you like (bait), cannot resist the temptation to fulfill your desires (lust), and go after the things you like without considering the costs or consequences (trap).

Most people cannot recognize the traps until after they have fallen victim to them. A shoplifter can detect hidden cameras, plainclothes security, and security attachments on clothes only because they have been caught stealing or because someone else taught them the game. Crime, rebellion, and disobedience are all acts of the flesh that we know to be sin against God (Romans 7:25). Remember the Adamic nature discussed in the first chapter? Fleshly, or carnal, nature is the same thing.

What is carnal nature? Within the human flesh is the invisible principle of sin called carnal nature. Mankind inherited this animal instinct from our first father on Earth, Adam. When our judgments and decisions are based only on our sensual desires, we are governed by animal instincts or controlled by animal appetites. An animal knows the foods it likes. The only way to find out if the food is not poisoned or is not a trap is to eat it first. Carnal nature also lures humans into traps the same way animals are captured (Romans 8:6).

The good news is, if animals can learn to resist the temptation of eating their favorite foods once they recognize the traps, so can we! We can avoid falling into traps by watching others become captured. It's all over television: *Bait Car*, *Cops*, *First 48*, *Teen Mom*, and *Intervention*, to name a few. The next time someone tries to lure you into sin or draw you away from your good nature, do not focus on how desirable the bait is. Beware of the trap!

Let's identify certain characteristics that could lure you into a trap so that you are able to resist temptation. Be aware that temptation has many forms that may not be easily recognized.

1. Taking shortcuts. How many times have you raced to finish something? In the end, you did a poor job and had to redo it. It cost you more time and energy to clean up your mistakes than to have done it right the first time. People cannot trust you to be responsible.

2. Not following instructions or failure to read the rules. How many times have you assumed you knew what to do? In the end, your performance was poor or you did not finish the job because you had no idea how much more you needed to learn. You end up feeling stupid.

3. Changing your normal routine to follow others. How many times has someone told you to go somewhere or to do something you would never do? In the end, you discovered that the person you listened to did not have a clue as to what they were talking about, and you both suffered the consequences.

4. Allowing others to speak for you. How many times has someone spoken up on your behalf without your saying how you really felt? In the end, others may have gotten the wrong impression about who you really are. You were then left to defend what should not have been said.

Temptation is usually disguised as something that's much easier, more enjoyable, faster, the only option, more profitable, worry-free, free of charge, undetectable, foolproof, better than ever, and so on. Think before you act!

Remember, God made a promise to save you. God cannot lie (Titus 1:2), but it's still your choice to resist flirting with sin and Satan, who tempts you (James 4:7; 1 Corinthians 10:13). Do not enter into Satan's battleground or you will lose the fight against temptation. For example, if your weakness is smoking, do not hang out with smokers, and avoid places where students are free to smoke. You would not see a person who is trying to lose weight hanging out at the donut shop; the temptation would be irresistible. Identify your temptations. Remove yourself from those people and surroundings that take advantage of your weaknesses.

Satan uses three major forms of temptation to take advantage of our desires and tempt us into sin: lust of the flesh, lust of the eyes, and the pride of life (1 John 2:16). This is Satan's oldest trick in the book. Eve fell into this trap when she disobeyed God by eating from the Tree of Knowledge of Good and Evil (Genesis 2:16-17).

The first deceitful method Satan used to tempt Eve was to minimize and disregard her punishment for disobedience. He told her, "You shall not surely die" (Genesis 3:4). Look for the trap whenever someone is tempting you to deny, debate, or minimize your punishment for pursuing your desires. These people will use phrases like, "You won't get caught" or "It's worth the risk." Know that if there is a slight possibility your actions warrant punishment, don't do it!

The second deceitful method Satan used to tempt Eve was to suggest that God was hindering Eve from becoming a god herself (Genesis 3:5). God knew that Eve's knowledge of good and evil would cause the fall of mankind, but Eve's pride likely caused her to make an attempt to overtake authority as a god. Look for the trap whenever someone is tempting you to turn against authority (parents/teachers) or to falsely accuse others. Those who tempt you may use phrases like, "Your parents are hating on you" or "Your teacher is discriminating against your race." Know that if you have to rebel against authority, don't do it!

In the end, Eve made the choice to disobey God. And the Devil did not make her do it! He only tempted her with her strongest desire, lust of the eyes (Genesis 3:6), and Eve ate from the tree and shared her fall into temptation with Adam. Criminals do the same thing when they recruit a "co-defendant" or "fall partner" to participate in sin.

Adam and Eve also made an attempt to cover up their sin (Genesis 3:7). Everyone has tried to cover an act of sin. But just as God gave Adam and Eve an appropriate covering (Genesis 3:21), God will also cleanse us from sin when we choose to repent (1 John 1:9). Look for the trap whenever someone's is tempting you to blame others and cover up your actions. These people will offer an alibi to convince you that you can get away with sin. They may also offer a scapegoat, or someone else to blame for your sin. Know that if you have to lie or blame someone else for your actions, don't do it!

Let's review some examples of how your worldly desires and fleshly lusts make it difficult to resist temptation.

Pride of Life

Have you ever met a pretty girl who only dates fellas who are violent and no good to her? Meet Tanya. She is eye candy and seems to have it going on, until you meet her boyfriend. Tanya is dating Johnny, a gang member who wears a natural mean-mug. The only thing Johnny is good at is knocking out boys. So why does Tanya date Johnny? She is controlled by her *pride of life*. Tanya looks sweet and innocent on the outside, but actually she thinks she knows everything and is very conceited (Proverbs 26:12). Tanya likes Johnny because he can protect her when she pretends to be more than what she really is (Galatians 6:3).

One day, a boy named Mike asked Tanya for her phone number. Tanya gladly exchanged numbers, but she gave Mike's number to her jealous boyfriend, Johnny. Mike went to the hospital and Johnny went straight to juvenile hall for assault. While Johnny was locked up, he thought Tanya was cheating. As soon as Johnny was released from jail, he rushed to speak with Tanya, but Johnny did all the talking with his hands. Tanya skipped school for a week to hide her black eye.

Tanya's pride would not allow her to face all her classmates who laughed and talked behind her back. She also avoided her parents, as Mom and Dad had warned her about dating thugs, but she would not listen. Tanya's pride caused her to continue dating Johnny just to prove she could change him. Besides, Johnny apologized, claiming he hit Tanya out of love (1 Corinthians 13:4-8) and promised to never hit her again. Too bad Tanya was controlled by her pride of life, because the day she stood up to Johnny, he broke his promise along with Tanya's jaw.

Lust of the Eyes

Have you ever met a church boy who had the lifestyle of a dope boy? Meet Gabriel. Everybody in Gabriel's family loves Jesus. Gabriel appears to be a humble servant of the Lord, until he leaves church (Matthew 23:27). He speeds in the school parking lot just to be seen in his Tahoe with twenty-six-inch chrome rims. Gabriel only hangs with students who have nice rides and top-of-the-line gear (James 2:1-4). So why does Gabriel, a child of God, have to look so fly? Gabriel is controlled by his *lust of the eyes*. One day a hustler named Ricky decided to take advantage of Gabriel. Ricky drives a BMW and is twenty-three years old, but only hangs with teenagers. While cruising the strip, Ricky made sure that Gabriel saw his brand-new BMW 745LI—all the bait he needed to set Gabriel up for a fall. Gabriel immediately fell in love with Ricky's ride when he noticed the immaculate interior. What Gabriel did *not* see was that the Beamer was stolen.

Ricky invited Gabriel to roll with him for the weekend. Since Ricky dressed like most of the college students at Gabriel's church, Gabriel assumed that Ricky was harmless based on his outward appearance (1 Samuel 16:7). Ricky's BMW swerved in both lanes as Gabriel trailed close behind. The cars stopped at a red light. While Gabriel was busy admiring the nice rides on the strip, a gunman pulled alongside and demanded his Tahoe. The BMW and Tahoe sped off as Gabriel stood in the street, wondering why he did not see the jack move coming (2 Corinthians 5:7).

Lust of the Flesh

Have you ever met a girl who was rumored to be a tease and had a bad reputation for *not* having sex? Meet Jill. She is outgoing, fun-loving, and easy to get along with. Jill has many friends on her Facebook page, but she has never had a boyfriend. So why does Jill have a bad rep for not having sex? Most of Jill's Internet buddies are controlled by their *lust of the flesh*. Jill has made the correct choice to not date because she has a personal relationship with Jesus Christ. The only relationships her friends have are chatting online, sexting, or hanging out late at night (Romans 8:4).

Friday was game day, and Jill and the rest of the cheerleaders wore their uniforms to school. Todd, who is driven by his out-of-control hormones, decided to locate Jill on Facebook. They chatted online only once, but Todd lied to his friends about Jill being unable to resist hooking up with him on the first night. Jill thought Todd was cool, but before she agreed to accept his friendship, Jill asked Todd if he knew Jesus. Todd never returned her text to confirm that he was a child of God (Matthew 10:32-33).

Todd became angry with Jill because she threw God in his face, so he e-mailed his friends, claiming that Jill was a tease and scared to go all the way. Jill was confused; she could not understand why boys were turned off by her being a Christian (Romans 8:6-7; 1 Corinthians 2:14). One day Jill will realize that she has the best relationship of all—a spirit-led connection with God. The power of the Holy Spirit enables Jill to resist falling into a lustful trap with the Devil.

Who Am I?

The following is an evaluation to help you pinpoint your lustful desires. The only way to resist temptation is through the power of the Holy Spirit. You must be able to identify the bait Satan uses to lure you into a trap.

Pride of Life

Would you be mad if your best friend showed up at your birthday party dressed better than you?

Do you always have to be first or cut in line to receive something?

Is pleasing your friend more important than doing what's best for you?

Have you had a fight or an argument because someone looked like they had a problem with you?

Do you hate it when your parents help you more than they need to?

If you answered yes to at least three of these questions, beware of falling into temptation due to your *pride of life*.

Lust of the Flesh

Do you easily make friends with attractive people but have trouble getting along with unattractive persons?

Does dressing your best mean you have to look sexy, show skin, or reveal the shape of your body?

When your parents give you advice about dating or sex, do you feel they are invading your privacy?

Do most of your friendships lead to dating?

Would you date more than one person at a time?

If you answered yes to at least three questions, beware of falling into temptation due to your *lust of the flesh*.

Lust of the Eyes

Can you look at the cover of a book, CD, or DVD and know for sure that you will like it or not be interested?

Have you ever ignored a person until you saw them with something you wanted?

Does a person's trend and style impress you more than their conduct and character?

Do you love reality shows but hate educational programs that are not entertaining?

Can you look at a person and tell if they are smart or dumb, tough or weak, rich or poor?

If you answered yes to at least three questions, beware of falling into temptation due to your *lust of the eyes.*

Correction and discipline is not to embarrass you by exploiting your weaknesses but to prevent you from being exposed by your weaknesses. Rules and instructions teach you to resist temptation so that you are equipped to walk in true repentance. The body of Christ supports all new believers as they journey through a new walk of life. It may get difficult, but God will provide you with options that will benefit you in the long run (1 Corinthians 10:13).

Lesson 3.2 Review

Multiple Choice

1. _____ cannot be tempted with evil, neither can he tempt any man with evil (James 1:13).
   A. A pastor   B. An usher   C. God   D. A judge
2. Satan draws us into traps by the lust of our flesh, eyes, and our _____ (1 John 2:16).
   A. Pride of life   B. Friends   C. Ghettos   D. Poverty
3. Adam and Eve sinned by eating from the Tree of _____ (Genesis 2:16-17).
   A. Life   B. Death   C. Money
   D. Knowledge of Good and Evil
4. "To be carnally [sinful] minded is _____; but to be spiritually minded is life and peace" (Romans 8:6, brackets added).
   A. Life   B. Death   C. Helpful   D. Evil

True/False

1. Those who are in the flesh cannot please God (Romans 8:8).
2. Satan is known as the prince of this world (John 12:31).
3. You can love the material things in this world just as much as you love God (1 John 2:15).
4. There is more hope for a conceited (prideful) man than a fool (Proverbs 26:12).

Fill in the Blank

1. "Every man is tempted when he is drawn away of his own _____, and enticed [trapped] (James 1:14, brackets added).
2. "Submit yourselves to God, _____ the devil, and he will flee from you (James 4:7).
3. God promised _____ _____, and God cannot lie (Titus 1:2).

4. Eve blamed _____ when she sinned in the Garden of Eden (Genesis 3:13).

5. The prophet named _____ made the mistake of choosing the king of Israel based on outward appearance, but God looks at the heart (1 Samuel 16:7).

6. You are not in the _____, but in the Spirit: The Spirit of God lives in you. If you do not have the Spirit of Christ, you are not a child of God (Romans 8:9).

Check Yourself

✓ Name one not-so-good person or thing you desire the most?
✓ Can you live without him/her/it?
✓ What can you do to prevent falling into temptation because of your strong desires?

CHAPTER 4

CLAIMING THE VICTORY!

Moral Lesson

I began wrestling my freshman year of high school. When I faced off with my first opponent, I got pinned in one minute. Coach said, "You looked weak. You gotta get stronger if you wanna win." I pumped iron and did more strengthening exercises. In my next match, I manhandled the boy at first. But halfway through the match, I could not get my hands on him. Coach said, "You looked slow. You gotta get faster if you wanna win."

By my third wrestling match, I was fast as lightning and was ahead on points after two periods. In the final period, I ran out of gas. Coach said, "You looked tired. You gotta have stamina and endurance if you wanna win." I was frustrated and wanted to win so badly, so I trained harder, improved my diet, and ran more.

In my fourth match, with one minute remaining, I found myself on my back. I used all the techniques, and still I was about to lose. The crowd yelled "Get up!" as coach counted down the final seconds. Somehow, I flipped the guy over and earned two points to win the match. Coach said, "You showed a lot of heart out there, son! You gotta be confident enough to claim your victory if you wanna keep winning."

Thank God that victory in the kingdom of heaven is not like sports. Jesus claimed the victory over sin the day he laid his life down on Calvary and died for the forgiveness of our sins (1 Corinthians 15:57-58). Your victory over sin was not because of your hard work and intense training, but by the mercy and grace of God (Titus 3:5). You claimed your victory by believing in Christ Jesus!

It is up to you to walk as a winner in God's kingdom. Show team spirit by praising the Lord the same way fans proclaim their loyalty. You reclaim your victory every time you remain faithful and resist temptation (1 John 5:4). Show the spirit of a champion by helping others. Enjoy a come-from-behind victory over sin each time you repent. As a follower of Christ, your life is an endless winning streak because Jesus came in the flesh to destroy the works of the Devil. Consult with Coach Jesus if you stumble or doubt. Study your playbook, the Bible, and you never have to fall (2 Peter 1:5-10).

4.1 Bearing Your Cross

Moral Lesson

My father got paid every two weeks. He gave me allowance with advice on how to manage my money until next payday. Dad said, "I can only take you so far. You gotta carry your own weight, son." *Yeah, whatever*, I said to myself, and I was out the door in a hurry.

I hung out with my friends usually until I was broke. Then Dad would come in and see me alone. Shaking his head, he'd say, "I see your friends were too heavy for you, huh?"

When my parents went out, they left my younger brother and me home alone. They always reminded me that I was in charge. Dad repeated those same safety tips and warnings. As my dad walked out the door, he'd say, "I can only take you so far. You gotta carry your own weight, son." I hardly paid attention, knowing that being home alone meant it was time to do whatever I wanted.

One time when our parents were gone, my brother and I fell asleep while preparing a late night snack. Dad woke me up as the smoke alarm blared and the stench of scorched noodles clouded the house. Shaking his head as he opened the windows, Dad said, "Responsibility weighed you down, huh, son?"

As a believer in Christ, you must carry your own weight. Learn self-control, restraint, and deny yourself things you do not need. A burden is simply a heavy weight to carry, which may be difficult to do. Being a Christian is only burdensome when you do not like to be corrected, follow instructions, or improve your behavior. The Scriptures teach us to bear our own burdens (Galatians 6:5). The most important burden that was lifted off your chest when you turned to Christ was dying in sin and going to hell! Now it is up to you to discipline yourself from desires that lead to prison, self-inflicted wounds, hate, or rebellion.

As you learn to be more Christ-like, you also discover that the burden of Christ is a light weight to carry (Matthew 11:28). The heavy loads that can darken your mood or steal your joy may be negative self-talk, unwillingness to change, or unwillingness to participate in school or church activities. Those you socialize with can really weigh you down with gossip, jealousy, peer pressure, and criticism.

To fully understand the weight of sin, compare it to the law of gravity: What goes up must come down. Sin will pull you down like a jar falling from the countertop or a plane crashing from the sky. Our flesh (sinful nature) binds us to sin the same way the earth subjects us to the law of gravity. At any time, you could fall due to lustful desires, poor judgment, or bad advice. But you are not alone. All Christians face similar challenges and temptations. That is why we are to bear one another's' burdens (Galatians 6:2).

Have a support group that gives positive feedback and healthy advice when you backslide or consider making a bad choice. Did you know that Christ needed help bearing his cross as he carried the weight of our sin to be crucified? (Matthew 27:27-32). Simon the Cyrene, who helped Jesus carry his cross, could only take him so far. Then Jesus had to bear the weight of our sin on his own (Hebrews 9:28).

You cannot measure the weight of sin, and you are not strong enough to carry sin, no matter how well you hide your sinful nature. But you can bear your own cross because Jesus commanded you to do so (Luke 14:27). The cross represents death. Ever heard the song by Justin Timberlake and T.I., "The Old Me is Dead and Gone"? Now that you live for Christ, your old habits and thoughts of sin are dead. You are born again into a person who is able to carry your cross on a daily basis. You carry your cross by asking forgiveness and forgiving others, praying for things out of your control, loving those who may not deserve it, and doing the right thing even when no one is watching.

You may have to bear the weight of avoiding friends and family who are not Christ-like (Romans 16:17-18; 2 Thessalonians 3:14-15). Your faith will be tested, but by remaining faithful in the worst of times or under severe peer pressure, you will purify your soul (1 Peter 1:7, 22). Bear your cross and claim your victory in Christ by learning self-control. Stop complaining about what you do not have and be thankful for what you *do* have.

You must be more than a church member on Sundays to bear your cross. You must have your own Bible. Simply ask your church for a Bible if you cannot afford one. Ask for a New King James Version or the New International Version or Amplified Bible if you have trouble reading the Old English style of writing in the King James Version. Bearing your cross is similar to a soldier making his final run to the Blackhawk helicopter, heading for safety. You may be under heavy attack, but your victory is within reach as fellow soldiers in Christ support your struggles.

As a soldier in God's army, always carry your weapons and ammo: the Spirit of God and the Bible. Eat some rations when you feel weak, i.e., read the Word and listen to it. Use your heavenly radio to communicate to your Commander, i.e., pray to God. Keep your survival kit handy in case you are injured on the battlefield: repent and seek counsel from men and women of God. And you may have to carry a wounded soldier to safety, i.e., encourage and help others when they need you the most.

To improve as Christ's disciple, you must count the cost of your actions. In other words, think ahead, and know your duties and responsibilities. Abide by rules at home and school and obey the law. You must plan for the unexpected. Do not be enticed by those flirting with you and resist those offering you drugs, alcohol, or cigarettes. Know the consequences and punishments: in-school detention/suspension, grounded, jail, injury, or death. And acknowledge the rewards of obedience: graduate from high school, get a job/allowance, and attend college.

To bear your cross also means to have mental toughness. You may struggle, get tired, or suffer. But to claim your victory, you have to win on the battlefield of your mind. Determination, dedication, and belief gives you heart to endure hard times when you would rather quit. Suffering unfortunate circumstances builds you up as a perfect, stronger Christian (James 1:2-4). You are in basic training. Do not second-guess making the correct choices even though you suffer losses. Do not blame yourself for parental neglect or abuse. Do not allow previous bad experiences to kill your hope and expectation for good. Do not beat yourself up for mistakes and poor decisions you cannot undo. The same high level of commitment and sacrifice needed to move up the military ranks is also required to grow in spirit and truth.

Confession

As a senior in high school, I caught a felony drug charge, but the judge agreed to dismiss my charge on my verbal commitment to graduate and enlist in the military. Graduating from high school was no problem, and a military recruiter inspired me to join the Marines. I passed the ASVAB written exam, but I needed X-rays for medical clearance due to a broken arm I suffered in ninth grade. My X-rays were difficult to locate, so eventually, I got cold feet and backed out of joining the Marines. Thank God, because the Persian Gulf War began shortly after I graduated. Lord knows I was not mentally tough enough to fight for my country.

The Lord will not send his soldiers into battle unprepared. In Exodus 13:17, God led his people the long way around the land of the Philistines, who would certainly attack Israel. God protected his people by not leading them into a war zone and their being tempted to turn back in fear to Egypt away from the Promised Land. God did not allow my medical clearance because I was so unstable that I may have gotten a fellow soldier or myself killed. But you do not have to be afraid of enlisting in God's military because the victory over Satan has been claimed by Christ's blood shed on the cross.

You have joined the most dominant military force! You may face the incoming fire of discrimination and disappointment and must know that grenades of temptation will be heaved your way. While marching on the battlefield, you must be mindful not to step on landmines of pride, greed, or doubt. In every war, hard times are very likely (2 Timothy 2:3-4). But you have been recruited to fight the good fight of faith (1 Timothy 6:11-12). Use your small arms of righteousness and humility. Take cover alongside tanks of faith and patience. Claim your victory over sin with spiritual weapons of mass destruction that cause explosions of deliverance and breakthroughs to success! Be watchful. Be sober. Be alert. Man up, soldier!

Lesson 4.1 Review

Multiple Choice

1. You have victory in _____ (1 Corinthians 15:57).
   A. Discipline   B. Hard work   C. Jesus   D. Teamwork
2. You are not saved by _____ but according to God's mercy and the washing and regeneration of the Holy Ghost (Titus 3:5).
   A. Faith   B. Works   C. Good deeds   D. Giving
3. You cannot serve both God and _____ (Matthew 6:24).
   A. Money   B. Jesus   C. Holy Ghost   D. Jehovah
4. Jesus said you should count the cost of being a disciple; prepare like a king prepares for _____ (Luke 14:31).
   A. Celebration   B. Death   C. Marriage   D. War
5. Fight the good fight of _____; take hold of eternal life (1 Timothy 6:12).
   A. Sin   B. Faith   C. Peer pressure   D. Youth

True/False

1. Jesus was so strong that he did not need help carrying his cross on the way to die for our sins (Matthew 27:27-32).
2. When you give your life to Christ, you must carry your own weight without help from others (Galatians 6:2, 5).
3. Christ chose to bear everyone's sins, and he will appear a second time without sin to take us to salvation (Hebrews 9:28).

Fill in the Blank

1. Jesus said, "Come to me all who labor and are heavy burdened, and I will give you _____" (Matthew 11:28).
2. Jesus said that if you do not bear his cross and follow him, you cannot be his _____ (Luke 14:27).
3. Endure hardness as a good _____ of Christ (2 Timothy 2:3).

Check Yourself

- ✓ What's the hardest thing you have to do at home or at school?
- ✓ What was the last thing you gave up on?
- ✓ Name one thing that you are struggling with, but you are willing to finish or hang on.

4.2 Warring With the Flesh

My dad is an ex-military man and is an enforcer of cleanliness. He told me all about his boot camp days and basic training in Germany. A high-ranking officer inspected their quarters daily with a fine-toothed comb. Any trace of dust, clutter, or disorder meant the entire troop suffered extra duties. I could not understand why soldiers were being trained to be neat-freaks.

My dad explained that cleanliness and order was a tactic of warfare. He said that a messy platoon could cost the lives of soldiers and result in a failed mission, as sloppiness was a sign of recklessness and carelessness. Soldiers could be tracked by the enemy if they left a mess from eating, smoking, bathing, or relieving themselves in the bushes. A neat, clutter-free camp made it easier to detect if the fort had been infiltrated when the troops were out scouting. Decency and order made it easy to spot if something was out of place or missing, as booby traps are more difficult to discover in a congested, trashed area.

We serve a God who is the master of decency and order (1 Corinthians 15:40). We must submit to the proper authority and obey the proper rules and procedures. Claim your victory over the Devil with a decent attitude, and keep your priorities in order. For example, making money is not your first priority. First, you must be educated. A college grad does an internship, which is working for free, to gain hands-on experience. Your chores and daily duties at home or school are your internships. You should not refuse to clean up or help out simply because you do not get paid.

As a soldier in Christ, your godliness is displayed in a clean and healthy lifestyle. Satan is your Enemy! He tracks filthy language, and you leave a trail for him to hunt you down every time you cuss, shout at your parents or elders, refusal to obey, or criticize others. Once Satan picks up your scent of *stinkin' thinkin'*, he will entrap you so deeply into sin that you will look down on others who are mindful to not use profanity. You may also lose respect for those who refrain from engaging in your negative conversations. Satan will trick you into *loving* explicit lyrics and hating clean versions of music or edited movies.

Please do not reject the truth nor take pleasure in unrighteousness. Or else, God may turn you over to the authority of Satan and judgment to hell (2 Thessalonians 2:7-12). You are in a full-blown war with your *flesh*. Your witness as a follower of Christ is at stake every time you face defining moments that others use to judge whether or not you are a Christian. For example, someone may cuss you out, and your *flesh* may entice you to also use foul language. Know that when others disrespect you, those are the moments when you truly identify yourself as a child of God or not. You do not have to back down, nor should you seek revenge. Rather, kill them with kindness (Romans 12:19-21). If you respond like the sinners, others will use that to define you as a faker and will say, "I told you so."

My teenage years of walking with Christ were very challenging. I knew not to lie, but what about when the truth meant telling on my friends and family? I knew not to deceive, but what should I have done when giving the facts would have caused Dad to beat Mom or encourage Mom to leave Dad? Do I ride home with drunken friends and risk dying in a collision or walk home and risk being shot or robbed? I remember many parties ending with gunshots. Why did I run toward the trouble instead of fleeing to safety?

Everyone goes through fleshly wars that may be confusing (Romans 7:22-23). You must fully understand what influences you to either win or lose the internal war that young believers face every day. We will examine the true essence of man and the divine order in which God created man. First, pray that God opens the eyes of your understanding. You have to rise above your normal patterns of thinking that are influenced by your feelings, experiences, and knowledge. Then, commit to following heavenly guidance no matter how different or difficult. It takes spiritual nourishment to empower you to claim your victory over your flesh.

Man's Divine Order of Influence

What is man? Man is spirit and was created in the likeness and image of God, who is Spirit (Genesis 1:27; Psalm 104:30; Romans 8:16). We know that the true essence of man is spirit and not this outer shell (flesh), because the Bible teaches us to worship God in spirit and in truth (John 4:24). You cannot determine worship or service to God by physical deeds alone. Why not? I can give someone something for the wrong reasons. I can pretend to bow my head in prayer, but I'm actually thinking negative thoughts. Your inner spirit and hidden intentions determine worship that is worthy to God. Man cannot judge your spirit and soul that cannot be seen, but God can (Hebrews 4:12).

Your spirit is your connection to God and must have more influence than your body, which is your carnal, Adamic nature or sensual desires. For example, your body may want sex outside of marriage or drugs. But your spirit teaches you to not destroy your body, which is the temple of God (1 Corinthians 3:16). The divine order teaches you to put your spirit first so that you keep your body holy instead of selling out for instant gratification or pleasures that could lead you into sin.

Note that there is a difference between the Holy Spirit of God (always spelled with a capital *S*) and the spirit of man (always spelled with a lowercase *s*). God created mankind, so everyone is a spirit. But only born-again believers in Christ have the presence of the Holy Spirit within them. What's the difference? Man's spirit generally wants to do what is morally right, but it also has its own attitude. Have you ever met a mean-spirited Christian? They exhibit tough love and zero tolerance. God uses those mean old Christians to instill discipline and order in stubborn, rebellious persons who usually do not respond to passive instruction. However, mean-spirited Christians tend to go overboard and may exhibit cold love through lack of compassion, mercy, and grace.

Man can also be poor in spirit, meaning he is humble, which is a blessing according to Jesus (Matthew 5:3). Man's spirit is flawed and has weaknesses because humans are not perfect. But the Holy Spirit of God is perfect. He allows believers to do things they normally could not do, such as resist temptation. I'm certain you have witnessed the delivering power of the Holy Spirit when someone suddenly quit smoking, left the gang, stopped fornicating (being promiscuous), and lost the attitude problem. The change may have been so drastic that it was impossible to believe.

As a born-again believer, your spirit is connected to the Holy Spirit, which gives you the victory in Christ Jesus. You win battles over Satan and your flesh because of the mercy and grace of God, not due to your own works or abilities. The problem is that mankind tends to forget that the flawless Holy Spirit is working through imperfect people. For example, a pastor or bishop may fall weak to temptation, and when he or she is exposed for sin, some of the congregation may deny that the head of the church was ever filled with the Holy Spirit. Others may give up their faith in God. Do not allow man's shortcomings to curse or deny the existence of God. If you do, your faith was never in God but in the charisma, personality, or showmanship of the person. Remember, the divine order is God first and everyone and everything else comes after.

"And God said, let *us* make man in our image, after our likeness . . ." (Genesis 1:26, emphasis added). Why did God say "us" and "our"? The plural form (reference of more than one) signifies the Holy Trinity of God's image as the Father (Jehovah), Son (Jesus), and Holy Spirit (Luke 1:35; Matthew 28:19; 1 John 5:7).

Yes, there is only one God, the Creator! God's true image established divine order when Jesus was born (Philippians 2:5-11). To win the war over your flesh, you must stay connected to God the Father. No one comes to the Father except by Jesus (1 John 14:6). The divine order of God cannot be changed (Matthew 28:19). Jesus instructs believers to pray to our heavenly Father (Matthew 6:9), and we are to close our prayers in the name of Jesus.

The Holy Spirit is last in the divine order because this form of God's manifest presence came after revelation of God the Father and God the Son, Jesus. Jesus promised the Holy Spirit would comfort us after he died (John 14:16, 26). The Holy Spirit signifies God is with us always. Once again, the divine order is God the Father, Son, and Holy Spirit (Matthew 28:19).

Let's analyze the creation of man. Mankind was created in the image and likeness of God but is not modeled after God according to nationality, race, or skin tone. Remember, God is Spirit. Therefore, mankind is spirit. We also have a divine order that is spirit, soul, and body (1 Thessalonians 5:23). Genesis 2:7 says, "The LORD God formed man of the dust of the ground, and breathed into his nostrils the breath of life; and man became a living soul." The dust of the ground is our body, which hosts our lower element (flesh) that can trap us in filth, or sin. The breath of God is our spirit (Psalm 104:29-30).

Claim the victory over sin by following the divine order that God intended for you. Your spirit must lead the soul, and your body must be in subjection (kept in self-control) by placing fleshly matters last to prevent you from being led into sin (1 Corinthians 9:27). Your spirit is your connection to God, so spiritual matters must always come before material and physical pleasures (Matthew 6:33).

Do not be discouraged if you do not completely understand the divine order of God and the true essence of man. You are young in spirit and faith. A seed has been planted that will grow as God reveals the truth to you. My investigations, facts, and personal revelations are not as effective at teaching as the Holy Spirit within you. Be patient. Pray continually. The more you submit to the will of God, the easier it is to win the war against the flesh.

Lesson 4.2 Review

Multiple Choice

1. The sinful nature that keeps a person trapped in disobedience, crime, or lust is in their _____ (Romans 7:23).
   A. Spirit   B. Peers   C. Body (members)   D. Enemies

2. Where is the law of God written so that you can know the right thing to do even when you are alone? (Jeremiah 31:31-33).
   A. Ten Commandments   B. Criminal law book
   C. Heart (spirit)   D. Internet

3. You must worship God in _____ (John 4:24).
   A. Body and soul   B. Church   C. Love
   D. Spirit and truth

True/False

1. All of mankind has a spirit, but only those who repent and become born-again believers in Christ have the Holy Spirit of God (Acts 2:38-39; Romans 8:14-16).

2. The spirit of man is his life principle breathed from God (Genesis 2:7).

3. When you live according to the Holy Spirit, you will always fulfill the lustful desires of the flesh (Galatians 5:16).

4. The flesh opposes the Spirit, but the Spirit and flesh are the same (Galatians 5:17).

5. Those who fulfill the lust of the flesh shall not inherit the kingdom of heaven (Galatians 5:21).

Fill in the Blank

1. Jesus promised a Comforter, which is the _____ _____, who God the Father sends to teach born-again believers all things (John 14:26).

2. God formed man from the dust of the ground, breathed life into him, and man became a living _____ (Genesis 2:7).

3. These are examples of works of the _____: fornication [unmarried sex], hatred, murder, and heresy [causing division] (Galatians 5:19-21).

4. These are _____ of the Spirit: love, peace, joy, longsuffering [patience], gentleness, goodness, faith, meekness, and temperance [self-control] (Galatians 5:22-23).

Check Yourself

- ✓ Does a voice in your head sometimes tell you to disobey or do bad things?
- ✓ Do you have good thoughts that prevent you from making bad decisions?
- ✓ Which voice do you listen to the most, the positive voice in your head or the negative one?

4.3 Winning in the Spirit

The creation of man is more complex than the physical body you see. Man is made of three elements: spirit, soul, and body.

Man's Spirit

What is the spirit of man?

1. Life principle (Genesis 2:7)
2. Conscious: moral qualities (Ezekiel 36:26-27)
3. Disposition: attitude/temper (Matthew 5:3; Proverbs 14:29; 16:18; 17:27)

The spirit is man's highest element because it is our connection to God. But because of our Adamic nature, man's spirit is naturally corrupted and unrighteous, which is why everyone needs to be born again in Christ Jesus.

Man's Soul

What is the soul of man?

1. Mind: intellect, imagination, ability to reason (Psalm 139:14; Proverbs 19:2)
2. Will: purpose, intention (Deuteronomy 11:13)
3. Emotions: feelings, desires, appetite, attitude (Job 10:1; 23:13)

The spirit and soul are similar because they are both immaterial (not physical; cannot be seen or touched). Only God truly knows what man thinks and can determine our intentions through our spirit and soul (Hebrews 4:12).

Man's Body

What is the body of man?

1. Members: body parts (Romans 6:12-13)
2. Five senses: hear, see, smell, touch, taste (Genesis 3:4-8)
3. Fleshly and sensual desires, immorality (Romans 7:18, 25)

Of course, man's body is the physical thing that we see. The body is man's lowest element because it holds the carnal, Adamic nature (Romans 7:23).

What happens to man's spirit, soul, and body once he or she dies? The spirit returns to God (Ecclesiastes 12:7), the body returns to the dust from which it was made (Genesis 3:19), and the soul faces eternal judgment for the choices made here on Earth (Proverbs 8:36; Acts 2:31; Hebrews 10:39; James 5:20). Please be very clear: Only the body dies! The spirit will return to God forever, and the soul will spend an eternity in heaven for those who are saved or an eternity in hell for those who are sinners.

How can a believer in Christ go against God's will and do what is obviously not right? Most decisions are based on how you think, the way you interpret, and what you envision as necessary. These are elements of your mind, which is within the soul. Other elements of your soul, such as your purpose, intentions, and emotions, also affect how your mind works and determine how you act. The logic and reasoning of your soul is influenced by either your spirit or your body, depending on which one is the strongest and most dominant.

As a believer in Christ, you should feed your spirit more than your body (fleshly nature). If not, you will more often be led by the lower elements of your flesh, which is the sinful nature of your body. For example, if you like music, listen to clean versions. Take note of how much time you spend watching television and watch only educational and informative shows. Be mindful that video games that promote crime and sex are not healthy. Realize that social networks online, such as Facebook, can be used to invade your privacy and spread rumors about you.

I strongly disagree with teen dating. However, if you must date, have one mate who is willing to get to know your ideas and goals instead of dating someone who is physically attracted to you. Do not lose sight of the fact that you should not be in a committed relationship that keeps you away from your loved ones and others who have your best interests in mind. You do not have to hang out after hours at places that are a risk to your well-being just to have fun. Church functions, school events, and family outings can all be exciting as long as you expect to have a good time.

Remember, those who are more influenced by the lustful desires of the body often feel justified because the end result of their sin is satisfaction and fulfillment of the flesh (2 Thessalonians 2:7-12). For example, as a teen, I had a lust for money. I watched thousands of poor people make lots of money that was not earned by working a legit job. So I reasoned that dealing drugs was the right thing to do. I believed that the only other option was to accept defeat or spend a lifetime working hard only to still be trapped in poverty. Besides, I thought that selling drugs could never be harmful considering how many people I was able to provide for.

However, I never considered the consequences of selling drugs because I was too blinded by my instant gratification. The end result was the crime carried much more time in jail than I realized, and I had helped create more drug addicts. I now realize that I contributed to the downfall of *crack heads* that neglected their children, sold their bodies, and harmed others to feed their drug habit.

If you are led by the lusts of your flesh and eyes the way I was, you are in serious need of divine transformation of your soul (Psalm 19:7). The only way to improve your thinking and lifestyle is to feed your spirit the proper nutrients: the Word of God, prayer, obedience, peace, and humility. Then your mind will logically lead your soul to connect with the spirit (Ephesians 4:23). Repentance will be sincere, and healthy choices will allow you to claim your victory in Christ (Romans 12:2).

The soul is a follower. Your spirit is the teacher or parent because of your connection to God, and your body is the bully using peer pressure to trap you into following the sinful nature. This is why pastors and other godly persons constantly preach about saving your soul. Even those who are saved and go to church regularly must make decisions every day to avoid the temptations of the flesh. A person who is controlled and dominated by fleshly lusts will refuse to repent or change their thinking although they may be active in church. Why? Because they constantly do things to feed the body, such as lie, steal, deceive, commit crime, envy, hate, etc.

Anyone who knows right from wrong and fully understands the consequences of sin yet continues to live a lifestyle of sin is in desperate need of a close encounter with God, e.g., near-death experience, imprisonment, total failure (business, relational, academic), abandonment by loved ones, or loss of what is desired most. I will not give up on anyone who is caught up in sin, and neither should you. Why? God may use you to draw a sinner into the kingdom of heaven (James 5:20).

Believers who have experienced godly sorrow of repentance will choose to follow Christ no matter how much temptation comes from their fleshly nature. Why? Their spirit has given power and dominance over their soul to the Holy Spirit. Sure, this person may have negative thoughts and he or she will have to make tough decisions to avoid sin every day. But this believer is maturing and has accepted that he was born to claim the victory over sin through the mercy and grace of God (2 Thessalonians 2:13-17).

You cannot win in the spirit unless you fully understand that the divine order of influence for born-again believers is spirit, soul, and body (1 Thessalonians 5:23). This is known as the regenerative state of man, which makes us alive in Christ and dead to sin (Titus 3:5). By maintaining the divine order, you are sanctified (set apart) and considered blameless by the mercy and grace of Christ.

Every day you may have sinful thoughts at least once. Immediately turn from what is tempting you and pray. If you do not, the gateway to sin is opened by your bad thoughts (Proverbs 23:7; 24:9). Remove yourself from the person, thing, or situation before you fall into sin (James 1:12-15).

My young brothers and sisters, I am not judging you. I come in love. My goal is to help you break free from the shackles that God freed me from. I understand there are many traps and temptations, such as violence, rebellion, laziness, selfishness, lying, and profanity. I empathize with your potential addictions of smoking, drugs, alcohol, or sex. I am compassionate for your delivery from those strongholds that are pulling you from claiming your victory in Christ: pride, entitlement, and unwillingness to forgive.

You can do it! Let go, and let God.

Lesson 4.3 Review

Multiple Choice

1. Only _____ can divide [separate] the soul and spirit and know the thoughts and intentions of your heart (Hebrews 4:12).
   A. You   B. God   C. Parents   D. Preachers
2. Jesus uses _____ as a metaphor for the Holy Spirit and knowledge of God, by which you are saved (John 4:14).
   A. Water   B. Tree   C. Vine   D. Salt
3. God says that all _____ are his, and the one that sins shall die (Ezekiel 18:4).
   A. Witches   B. Souls   C. Demons   D. Spirits
4. The _____ of foolishness is sin (Proverbs 24:9).
   A. Sight   B. Sound   C. Thought   D. Touch
5. Love, peace, and joy are fruits of the _____ (Galatians 5:22).
   A. Body   B. Soul   C. Mind   D. Spirit

True/False

1. Bitterness is not a feeling within the soul (Job 10:1).
2. The three parts of man are spirit, soul, and body (1 Thessalonians 5:23).
3. You will never fall if you keep adding to your faith virtue [truth], knowledge, self-control, patience, and godliness (1 Peter 1:5-10, brackets added).
4. Some angels left heaven and are now in everlasting chains of darkness waiting to be judged (Jude 6).

Fill in the Blank

1. If the _____ be without knowledge, it is not good (Proverbs 19:2).
2. Be _____ in the spirit of your mind for repentance/change (Ephesians 4:23).

3. "And fear not them which kill the body, but are not able to kill the _____: But rather fear him [God] which is able to destroy both _____ and body in hell" (Matthew 10:28, brackets added).

4. When you die, your body goes back to the dust (earth). Your _____ returns to God who gave it to you (Ecclesiastes 12:7).

Check Yourself

- ✓ Name one thing you do that keeps you close to God.
- ✓ Are you trapped in a bad habit or relationship from which you need the power of God to set you free?
- ✓ Do you pray and believe that the Holy Spirit will help you?

CHAPTER 5

KNOWING THE HISTORY OF SALVATION AND OUR SAVIOR, JESUS CHRIST

When I first got saved, I knew in my heart that Jesus was real and truly believed that God's promise of salvation to all mankind was true. But I was confused, because I could not understand how Jesus could be both God and the Son of God. Well, I also did not understand electricity, but that did not prevent me from using electrical appliances or believing there was an energy source making those appliances work.

As a young believer, you should not allow your lack of spiritual understanding to cause you to doubt what you believe to be true. Jesus is both the Son of God (Luke 1:35) and the everlasting Father (Isaiah 9:6). This lesson will help you fully understand that there is one God in a three-part being: Father, Son, and Holy Spirit (Matthew 28:19; 1 John 5:7), and that Jesus came to shed blood for the forgiveness of our sins (Hebrews 9:22). You will also learn that Jesus existed before the foundation of the world(John 8:53-58), and that the birth of Jesus was also one-third of the Godhead manifested on Earth as a human example for us of an obedient, humble servant of God till death (Philippians 2:5-11).

Take note of what God the Father says about Jesus Christ in Hebrews 1:8, "But unto the Son, he saith, 'Thy throne, O God, is forever and ever.'" The beginning of Hebrews 1 confirms the chapter as the spoken Word of God.

I always wondered what color Jesus was. Some churches have pictures of Jesus as a white man, while others portray him as a Jew. But in my church and in my home, Jesus was black. But it is not for us to argue whether Jesus' skin was light or dark. The undeniable truth is that Jesus was born in Bethlehem of Judea known today as the Middle East and was known as "The King of the Jews" (Matthew 2:1-2). However, Scripture does not confirm Jesus' skin tone. In theory, one may determine that Jesus looks like any Jew of today, but all Jews do not look alike, as climate affects skin tone.

Mankind is at liberty to portray Jesus' skin tone as a reflection of their individual race. What is more important is that we are all creations of God and are called to be Christ-like (Romans 8:28-31). If you choose to portray Jesus as your own race for motivation to do the will of God, then that's your choice. (Matthew 12:50).

5.1 Abrahamic Covenant

God's promise of salvation was first to the Hebrews (Jews) and then all of mankind also received the promise (Romans 1:16; Titus 2:11). We must go to the Old Testament to track God's first covenant [agreement] with Abraham. Then we can trace how the promise of salvation came through Jesus Christ. The promise to Abraham's seed in the Old Testament was an earthly foreshadow of God's promise to believers in Christ to inherit the kingdom of heaven (Galatians 3:16-29).

For example, let's say I promise to fly all teens from the United States to the moon, but then teens from every country relocate to the United States to become citizens. However, when it is time to fill the space shuttle, I will uphold my promise first to those teens I made the covenant with and then I will fly the new immigrants to the moon. Understand that God did not show favoritism to the Jews but simply kept his promise to those with whom he first made the agreement.

Who was our father Abraham who we used to sing about in church? Abraham was a Hebrew (Genesis 14:13), or rather a Jew. God promised Abraham that he would make his seed a great nation (Genesis 17:1-27). The Abrahamic covenant was God's promise to deliver Abraham and his people (the Hebrews) to a land called Canaan, which was plentiful and flowed with milk and honey. God also promised to multiply Abraham's seed, and that his children for generations to come would also inherit the promised land of Canaan for an everlasting possession (Genesis 17:1-2, 7-8).

Abraham had two sons, Ishmael and Isaac (Genesis 16:3-4, 16), but God's covenant was with Isaac, Abraham's younger son (Genesis 17:9, 19-21). Isaac had twin sons, Esau and Jacob (Genesis 25:21-26). God later changed Jacob's name to Israel (Genesis 32:28; 35:10), who became the father (patriarch) of the twelve tribes of Israel.

One of Israel's sons was named Judah (Genesis 35:23). Through the tribe of Judah came King David, and twenty-eight generations later, Jesus was born (Matthew 1:17; Hebrews 7:14). God appointed Jesus to reign over the house of Jacob (Israel) forever, and there would be no end to his kingdom (Luke 1:31-33).

Lesson 5.1 Review

Multiple Choice

1. God promised to make Abraham a great nation and established a _____ with Abraham's seed forever (Genesis 17:12-7).
   A. Peace treaty   B. War   C. Pardon   D. Covenant
2. _____ was Abraham's firstborn son, but God's promise was to Isaac, the son of Sarah (Genesis 16:3-4, 16; 17:20-21).
   A. Ishmael   B. Israel   C. Jacob   D. Joseph
3. God promised Abraham and his seed this land possession forever (Genesis 17:1-8).
   A. Egypt   B. Canaan   C. Babylon   D. Africa
4. Jesus was born through which tribe of Israel (Hebrews 7:14)?
   A. Reuben   B. Benjamin   C. Judah   D. Levi

True/False

1. Isaac had twin brothers named Esau and Jacob (Genesis 25:21-26).
2. Esau is the father of the twelve tribes of Israel (Genesis 35:23-26).
3. These are names given to Jesus: Wonderful, Counselor, the Mighty God, the Everlasting Father, and the Prince of Peace (Isaiah 9:6).

Fill in the Blank

1. God made a promise to Abraham and his seed. Abraham's seed is _____ (Galatians 3:16-17).
2. _____ was one hundred years old when he and his wife had a child (Genesis 17:10, 17).

Check Yourself

- ✓ Has anyone ever broken a promise to you?
- ✓ Have you ever made a promise that you knew you could not keep?
- ✓ Will you consider the sacrifices you have to make before you make the next promise?

5.2 New Covenant

In the Old Testament [covenant], the children of Israel sacrificed lambs, bulls, and rams as an offering to God to repent for their sins, as without the shedding of blood there could be no remission [forgiveness] of sin (Hebrews 9:22, brackets added). God gave Jesus, his only begotten Son, as a perfect sacrifice to purify us from the filthiness of our flesh and Adamic nature (Hebrews 9:11-14).

The new covenant is much better because we are under the mercy and grace of God. God understands that due to our sinful nature we are likely to fall short of God's glory, so he wrote his law in our heart. As a result of God's new covenant, we have eternal life in heaven instead of a land possession promised to Abraham (Hebrews 8:6-13).

In the Old Testament, Pharaoh held the children of Israel captive in Egypt. In order to deliver his chosen people to the Promised Land, the LORD sent ten plagues on Egypt as Moses pleaded with Pharaoh, "Let my people go!" (Exodus 5:1-3; 9:1-14) The tenth and final plague was called the Passover, where God sent his death angel to kill the firstborn male of each Egyptian family. But the Israelites were commanded to kill a spotless lamb and put its blood on their doorposts so that when the death angel saw the blood, he would know that God's chosen people were inside the home and would then pass over that house, sparing those children (Exodus 12:1-14).

Israel feasted on the lamb and ate unleavened bread [without yeast] once a year in remembrance of salvation and deliverance to the Promise Land of Canaan (Exodus 12). Today, Christ is our lamb that offered his pure blood as a one-time sacrifice for the forgiveness of our sins (John 1:29). On the night that Jesus was betrayed by Judas Iscariot and was seized to be crucified, Jesus celebrated the Jewish Passover (Matthew 26:1-5; 24-28) and ate with his disciples what is now known as the Lord's Supper.

There are two elements to partake of the Lord's Supper: bread and wine [grape juice]. The bread represents Christ's body, which was broken [crucified, pierced] for mankind, and the wine, which represents the new covenant of Jesus' blood that was shed for the forgiveness of mankind's sins (1 Corinthians 11:24-25). Jesus did not specify how often Christians should partake of the Lord's Supper, but as we do, we are to remember Jesus' death, burial, and resurrection.

> The promise of the new covenant is for you, and everyone who believes in Jesus. You made a choice to believe in Jesus, therefore, you are saved from eternal death in hell. You have gained everlasting life in heaven. Before you take the Lord's Supper, examine yourself. Forgive everyone that offended you as well as seek forgiveness. Confess your sins so that you are worthy to take the Lord's Supper (1 Corinthians 11:26-30; Mark 11:25).

> For God so loved the world that he gave his only begotten son, that whoever believes in him should not perish, but have everlasting life (John 3:16).

Lesson 5.2 Review

Multiple Choice

1. Jesus Christ died for us because without _____ there could be no forgiveness of sin (Hebrews 9:22).
   A. Man B. Bloodshed C. Jews D. Killing the innocent
2. John the Baptist called Jesus the _____ (John 1:29).
   A. Lamb of God   B. Tree of Life   C. Bird of Freedom
   D. Dove of Salvation
3. Jesus ate the Lord's Supper with his disciples. He blessed and broke the bread, saying, "Take, eat; this is my ____ broken for you. Do this in remembrance of me" (1 Corinthians 11:24).
   A. Leg   B. Hand   C. Foot   D. Body

True/False

1. Christ's blood was a perfect sacrifice to God instead of the blood of bulls, goats, or rams sacrificed in the Old Testament (Hebrews 9:11-14).
2. Christ brought an excellent ministry, but not better than the old covenant with Abraham (Hebrews 8:6-9).
3. Judas betrayed Jesus during the feast of the Jewish Passover now known as the Lord's Supper (Matthew 26:1-4, 24-28).

Fill in the Blank

1. God said that he would make a new _____. "I will put my laws into their mind, and write them in their hearts" (Hebrews 8:10).
2. Jesus held up a cup of wine and told his disciples, "Drink all of it; for this is my ____ of the new testament, which is shed for many the forgiveness of sins" (Matthew 26:28).
3. Jesus said, "When you stand praying, _____, if you have ought [problem] against any; that your Father in heaven may also _____ you" (Mark 11:25, brackets added).

4. Before taking the Lord's Supper, you should _____ yourself. It is condemnation [guilty] to eat and drink unworthily (1 Corinthians 11:24-30, brackets added).

Check Yourself

- ✓ Has someone ever promised you something and then gave you more than you expected?
- ✓ What was the last promise you fulfilled?
- ✓ Can you promise to be accountable for your own actions?

5.3 The Holy Trinity

What is the Trinity? And why isn't that word in the Bible?

The Bible is a translation of Hebrew (Old Testament) and Greek (New Testament) into Old English language. *Trinity* is a fairly new English word that did not exist when the Bible was translated, which is why it is not in the Bible. However, the concept of Trinity has existed since the beginning of creation. The Holy Trinity is God the Father, God the Son, God the Holy Spirit (Luke 1:35).

Words and phrases may change or originate over a period of time and through translation. However, newly formed words such as *Trinity* can be a derivative or variation of a preexisting word, concept, or principle. For example, the word *Christ* is not in the Old Testament. But, *Messiah* is the Hebrew word for the Greek word *Christ* (Daniel 9:24-26; Matthew 16:16). Both words, *Messiah* and *Christ*, identify Jesus, our Lord and Savior.

The book of Matthew is the only one of the four Gospels (Matthew, Mark, Luke, and John) to use the word *church* or *"ecclesia"* (Matthew 16:18; 18:17). The word *church* is not mentioned again until after the Pentecost in Acts 2:47. Does this mean that the church did not exist in Old Testament times? Certainly not! We get our word *church* from the following phrases: "house of the LORD" (Exodus 34:26), "tabernacle of the congregation" (Exodus 29:42), and "sanctuary" (Exodus 25:8).

Here's another example to help you better understand how the the Holy Trinity can be a truthful concept although not used in that exact phrase in the Bible. The word *Christian* is not mentioned in the Old Testament or the Gospels, as Christians were not formed until after Christ had gone to glory and they were established in Antioch (Acts 11:26). But Christians are the same as Jesus' disciples, or followers of Christ, and the Old Testament believers who sought the Messiah.

The Holy Trinity is an eternal biblical principle that refers to the three-part existence and manifestation of God, who is One (Ephesians 4:6; 1 John 5:7). Can Jesus be both God and the Son of God? Yes! Jesus is one-third of the Godhead (Colossians 2:8-10; 1 Timothy 3:16). The Trinity signifies divine order headed by God the Father, whose name is Jehovah (Exodus 6:3). (Note: For those who want more in-depth study, research the word *Elohim*, which translates as *God* in Genesis 1:1. The *im* ending signifies God's plurality, as the word *cherubim* is plural for angels (Psalm 18:10; 1 Samuel 4:4).)

Do I fully understand how God can be plural yet only be one? Not exactly because there is nothing physical that can be compared to God (Isaiah 40:18). But I do believe! It takes divine revelation from God to fully understand the Holy Trinity. My investigations may not be able to fully teach you, but a seed has been planted within you for God to open the eyes of your understanding when He says you are ready.

The Holy Trinity was outlined as Jesus taught his disciples, " . . . teach all nations, baptizing them in the name of the Father, and of the Son, and of the Holy Ghost" (Matthew 28:19). But only one man, Jesus, can save mankind from sin (Acts 4:10-12). Jesus is the beginning and the end (Revelation 1:8). "In the beginning was the word, and the word was with God, and the word was God . . . And the word was made flesh, and dwelled [lived] among us, (and we beheld his glory, the glory of the begotten of the Father) full of grace and truth" (John 1:1-2, 14, brackets added). We receive confirmation of the Trinity as the apostle John notes, "For there are three that bear record in heaven, the Father, the Word [Jesus, who became flesh], and the Holy Ghost: and these three are one" (1 John 5:7, brackets added).

Let's go back to the beginning when God created man (Adam). "And God said, 'Let *us* make man in *our* image, after *our* likeness . . .'" (Genesis 1:26, emphasis added). It's apparent that God made reference to Himself as the Creator, the Son of God (Jesus), and the Holy Ghost.

Philippians 2:5-11 confirms that Jesus is the form of God and equal to God, but also that he gave up his glory by taking on the form of a servant to be made in the likeness of man. Jesus was humble and remained obedient till death as an example of how we are to live. Christ also prayed to God the Father when he finished his work on Earth and prepared to reclaim his glory by returning to God the Father (John 17:1-5).

If you do not understand the Holy Trinity, I pray that God reveals it to you (Proverbs 3:3-5). I cannot make you see the deity (godliness, holiness) and humanity of Jesus, and my goal is not to force you to believe what you will not receive. I only aim to plant a seed of knowledge and truth based on healthy biblical teachings (1 John 5:10-12). Lord willing, other ministers will water this seed of reverence for the Holy Trinity and God will increase your understanding.

Lesson 5.3 Review

Multiple Choice

1. _____ said, "Let us make man in our image, after our likeness" (Genesis 1:26).
   A. Satan   B. Pharisees   C. God   D. Sadducees
2. At the name of _____, which is above every name, every knee shall bow and every tongue confess that he is Lord (Philippians 2:9-11).
   A. Jehovah   B. Jesus   C. Elijah   D. Moses
3. "Trust in the LORD with all your heart. Lean not on your own _____, but in all your ways acknowledge God and he will direct your ways" (Proverbs 3:5-6).
   A. Understanding   B. Power   C. Talents   D. Goals

True/False

1. The word *Trinity* is not in the Bible, but it simply refers to God the Father, Son, and Holy Spirit (Matthew 28:19).
2. There are many names of men that can save us besides Jesus (Acts 4:10-12).
3. Jesus said, "I am the alpha and omega, the beginning and end" (Revelation 1:8).
4. Jesus descended [came down] from heaven, and then he died, resurrected, and ascended [raised] back to heaven (Ephesians 4:7-10).

Fill in the Blank

1. God the almighty Father declared that his name is _____ (Exodus 6:3; Psalm 83:18).
2. Jesus said to teach all nations and _____ them in the name of the Father, Son, and Holy Spirit (Matthew 28:19).

3. Christ Jesus, being in the form of ____, made himself of no reputation and took on the form of a servant to be made in the likeness of men (Philippians 2:5-7).

Check Yourself

- ✓ Is there something about the Bible that you do not trust?
- ✓ Are you around a man or woman of God who helps build your faith?
- ✓ Will you choose to pray about the things that are out of your control?

The end of this text signifies the beginning of your newness of life in Christ!

Today the Lord is blessing you with an opportunity to be forgiven of your sins. Take your first step toward improving your future. Through faith in Christ Jesus, you can receive God's greatest gift: Eternal Life! *"For by grace are you saved through faith; and not of yourselves: it is the gift of God"* (Ephesians 2:8).

The Holy Spirit empowers you to resist temptation. You will soon **recognize God's voice within yourself**, and be encouraged to turn from sin, foresee trouble and avoid it. This text helps you learn the word of God and see yourself in a new light that your parents or teachers may not have explained. Re-think possible. Build your faith by following Jesus' perfect example, instead of counting on man's likelihood to let you down. Take a hold of God's favor that none of us deserves. It is your choice. Will you claim the victory? By opening this book you have agreed to open your heart to Christ.

What Must I Do To Be Saved is the inspired word of God tailor-made for teens and spiritual *babes*. The text contains testimonies, exhortations and moral lessons that portray common lifestyles of teenagers. Scriptural references provide basic fundamentals and teachings of salvation; faith; repentance.

The text is designed to build teen's awareness of God's presence within them. The internal battle of spirit versus flesh is identified to prepare youth to resist temptation and overcome obstacles. Each sub-topic concludes with a lesson review that consists of multiple choice, true/false, and fill-in-the-blank questions that have a scriptural reference to assist research and memorization of the Holy Scriptures. *Check Yourself* is provided to emphasize how the biblical teachings can be directly applied to individual circumstances, mind-sets, or developments.

Make that change! Choose to be set free from relational traps and locked-up mind-sets that steal your joy, peace, and freedom and become who God has called you to be. I pray this message leads you to God's purpose for your life. Do you believe?